# The Procrastinator's Guide to

# TAXES MADE EASY

# The Procrastinator's

## Guide to

# TAXES

# MADE EASY

## Grace W. Weinstein

**NEW AMERICAN LIBRARY**

NEW AMERICAN LIBRARY
Published by New American Library, a division of
Penguin Group (USA) Inc., 375 Hudson Street, New York, New York 10014, U.S.A.
Penguin Books Ltd, 80 Strand, London WC2R 0RL, England
Penguin Books Australia Ltd, 250 Camberwell Road,
Camberwell, Victoria 3124, Australia
Penguin Books Canada Ltd, 10 Alcorn Avenue, Toronto, Ontario, Canada M4V 3B2
Penguin Books (N.Z.) Ltd, Cnr Rosedale and Airborne Roads,
Albany, Auckland 1310, New Zealand

Penguin Books Ltd, Registered Offices: 80 Strand, London WC2R 0RL, England

First published by New American Library, a division of Penguin Group (USA) Inc.

First Printing, January 2004
10   9   8   7   6   5   4   3   2   1

 REGISTERED TRADEMARK—MARCA REGISTRADA

LIBRARY OF CONGRESS CATALOGING-IN-PUBLICATION DATA
Weinstein, Grace W.
   The procrastinator's guide to taxes made easy / Grace W. Weinstein.
      p.   cm.
   ISBN 0-451-21106-5
   1. Income tax—Law and legislation—United States—Popular works.   2. Tax
returns—United States—Popular works.   3. Tax planning—United States—Popular works.
   I. Title: Procrastinator's guide.   II. Title: Taxes made easy.   III. Title.
   KF6369.6.W445   2004
   343.7305'2—dc22            2003019325

Set in Sabon
Printed in the United States of America

PUBLISHER'S NOTE
This publication is designed to provide accurate and authoritative information in regard to the
subject matter covered. It is sold with the understanding that the publisher is not engaged in rendering legal, accounting or other professional services. If you require legal advice or other expert
assistance, you should seek the services of a competent professional.

While the author has made every effort to provide accurate telephone numbers and Internet addresses at the time of publication, neither the publisher nor the author assumes any responsibility
for errors, or for changes that occur after publication.

BOOKS ARE AVAILABLE AT QUANTITY DISCOUNTS WHEN USED TO PROMOTE
PRODUCTS OR SERVICES. FOR INFORMATION PLEASE WRITE TO PREMIUM MAR-
KETING DIVISION, PENGUIN GROUP (USA) INC., 375 HUDSON STREET, NEW YORK,
NEW YORK 10014.

For Steve, still

# ACKNOWLEDGMENTS

The author gratefully acknowledges the work of the many tax professionals and tax publishers who work so hard to interpret endlessly changing tax law and IRS regulations. A special vote of thanks goes to the dedicated staff at CCH Incorporated: Leslie Bonacum and Neil Allen fielded endless inquiries, and Glenn Borst and James Solheim diligently reviewed the manuscript for technical accuracy. Any oversights or omissions are the author's alone.

# DISCLAIMER

This book is designed to provide accurate and up-to-date information. But tax laws and regulations are extremely complicated and change on a regular basis. Readers also have individual needs that may not be addressed in a book providing an overview of complex issues. Since neither the author nor the publisher is engaged in rendering legal, accounting, or other professional services, we strongly recommend that you seek the services of a competent professional for specific tax information applicable to your individual circumstances. The author and the publisher expressly disclaim any liability or responsibility for any losses that may be sustained or are alleged to be sustained, directly or indirectly, by the use of the information in this book.

# CONTENTS

# INTRODUCTION

Are you a shoebox taxpayer? The shoebox taxpayer is the man or woman who marches into an accountant's office sometime in April, dumps a shoebox full of receipts on the desk, and asks to have a tax return ready to mail by April 15. The shoebox school also includes taxpayers putting off preparing their own returns until the very last moment, then scrambling to locate all the essential documents and receipts.

Whether you rely on a professional tax preparer or do your own tax returns, it's no surprise that you're building stress to outrageous levels by tackling taxes on the eve of the deadline.

You're also spending more money than you should. Tax preparation fees are higher for disorganized last-minute taxpayers than for those who present well-organized tax records. And waiting till the last minute means that you miss out on—or can't take maximum advantage of—some deductions and credits.

What's more, April 15 isn't the only "D day" for taxes. Estimated taxes are due each quarter. So are property taxes for homeowners. Miss some tax filing deadlines and you'll not only pay more in taxes, you may also owe fines and penalties.

There's a better way. Tax filing is a necessary evil—but it doesn't have to be a thoroughly unpleasant experience. Organizing tax data as you march through the year and tackling taxes in manageable installments, a little bit at a time, can help you:

- reduce the anxiety and stress associated with tax time
- get a better handle on your finances in general, and, as an added bonus
- reduce the amount you must pay in taxes while
- avoiding interest and penalties on late payments

*The Procrastinator's Guide to Taxes Made Easy* organizes the year—and your tax chores—month by month. Following this simple recipe will help you deal with taxes in manageable segments, in relatively little time, leaving you serene and well prepared to meet filing deadlines. It will also help you manage your money better, as tax-related savings opportunities crop up all through the year.

So take it a little bit at a time, digesting manageable pieces of information, and you'll be—if not a happy taxpayer (I can't work miracles!)—a stress-free taxpayer with more money in your pocket. Good luck!

**GRACE W. WEINSTEIN**

# First Quarter: Tax Basics

# CHAPTER 1

# January
## Getting Started

"Indoors or out, no one relaxes
In March, that month of wind and taxes.
The wind will presently disappear,
The taxes last us all the year."

"Thar She Blows," by Ogden Nash

When Ogden Nash wrote about March as "that month of wind and taxes," federal income tax returns were due on March 15. The due date may have shifted to April 15, but the sentiment remains the same. Taxes *do* "last us all the year." But by tackling your taxes bit by bit over the course of the year, you can come out the winner.

Procrastination is human nature. Faced with tasks that are time-consuming, tedious, and expensive to boot, who wouldn't delay?

But unpleasant tasks only loom larger when delayed. And waiting until spring to tackle tax preparation raises stress levels, creates unnecessary anxiety, and frequently costs money— money that is better in *your* pocket than in Uncle Sam's.

## The Price of Procrastination

Peter and Patty picked an accountant's name out of the Yellow Pages at the beginning of April, then marched into her office with a ragtag collection of pay stubs, receipts, and 1099 forms reporting miscellaneous income. The accountant, already busy with clients who planned ahead and without the time to sort through their shoebox of documents, was unable to complete their federal and state tax returns on time. With an automatic extension courtesy of Uncle Sam, the couple postponed filing their tax return until August 15. But, since they hadn't put aside the money to pay most of their tax bill in April—when it was due, regardless of extensions—they owed an additional $500 on their federal tax bill of $2,000. The penalty could have been avoided by planning ahead.

Oscar and Olivia, on the other hand, sat down early last December to review their tax situation and see what they could still do to cut their tax bill for the year. There was quite a bit they could do, starting with adding to their retirement plan contributions, making sure all required quarterly estimates had been paid on time and in the right amount, and prepaying their January mortgage bill and their first-quarter property taxes before the year ended. Taking these steps in December—and then starting the new year right by organizing tax-related receipts and documents as they come in—meant no penalties, no interest, and a lower tax bill.

And that's what this book is about. Getting organized—and staying organized throughout the year—will help you pay your taxes on time and avoid penalties and interest. It will also help you spot ways to reduce your tax bill through timely action.

The tax code is extremely complex—all 54,846 pages of it(!)—but you can leave the complexities to the legions of accountants and attorneys who specialize in its intricacies. You really do have a manageable task when it comes to doing your taxes and saving money. We'll start with the basics: First, we'll look at what is taxable income and what is not. Next, we'll examine the deductions and credits that can cut your tax bill. There are more than you might think possible.

---

## SOME KEY DATES IN U.S. TAX HISTORY

**1862:** The first income tax, at 3 percent, as an emergency measure to pay for the Civil War.

**1872:** The 1862 law is allowed to lapse.

**1894:** A 2 percent federal income tax enacted—and ruled unconstitutional by the U.S. Supreme Court in 1895

**1909:** A proposed 16th amendment to the U.S. Constitution authorizing Congress to collect taxes on income becomes law in 1913, when Wyoming casts the deciding vote. One in 271 people pays tax at 1 percent.

**1926:** The Revenue Act of 1926 reduces taxes because too much tax is being collected.

**1939:** Revenue statutes are codified. One out of thirty-one citizens now pays federal tax at 4 percent.

**1943:** Withholding on salaries and wages is introduced. One out of three people now pays federal income taxes.

**1954, 1969, 1984, 1986:** Monumental overhauls of the federal income-tax system.

**1996, 1997, 2001, 2002:** Major legislation changing the tax code.

(© 2003, CCH Incorporated. All Rights Reserved. Reprinted with permission.)

---

## Taxable and Nontaxable Income

Not surprisingly, the IRS offers up a lengthy list of taxable sources of income. As you would expect, the list includes salary and wages, interest and dividends, and business receipts. Nothing surprising here. But it also includes

- fees, commissions, and bonuses
- capital gains
- rental income
- royalties
- tips
- pensions, annuities, and retirement plan distributions
- alimony and maintenance payments if they are deducted by the payer
- prizes and awards
- some fringe benefits
- a portion of Social Security retirement benefits for some taxpayers
- unemployment compensation
- disability income if your employer paid the premiums

Make a profit on a tag sale? It, too, is reportable income. Win a bet on your favorite horse or clean up at the blackjack table, and you owe income tax on your winnings.

Some income, however, escapes the federal tax net and is yours to keep. Examples include

- interest on most municipal bonds and dividends paid by mutual funds holding such bonds
- profits on the sale of a home, up to $250,000 for a single taxpayer and $500,000 for a married couple filing jointly, so long as you have owned and lived in the house for two of the five years before the sale

- gifts and inheritances—although, once you put the money in the bank or invest it, the income it earns is taxable
- child-support payments
- life-insurance death benefits, including predeath benefits paid to terminally ill policyholders under policies with such provisions
- reimbursed business expenses
- worker's compensation
- disability income if you paid the premiums
- employer-paid health insurance or education assistance
- some or all of Social Security retirement benefits, depending on your income

## BREAKING THE CODE

- **"gross income"** includes everything that is taxable
- **"adjusted gross income (AGI)"** is gross income reduced by specific deductions including alimony, student loan interest, and deductible contributions to IRA, Keogh, and SEP retirement plans
- **"modified adjusted gross income (MAGI)"** is typically higher than AGI because it eliminates some tax breaks for certain calculations. For example, tax-exempt income from municipal bonds is included in MAGI in determining whether Social Security benefits are taxable
- **"taxable income,"** the amount on which you actually pay tax, is adjusted gross income reduced by personal exemptions and either the standard deduction or itemized deductions

# Deductions

Deductions reduce gross income, producing adjusted gross income (AGI). You have a choice. You may elect to take the standard deduction or itemized deductions, but you must do one or the other, not both.

## Standard Time

You can skip some calculations—and file a short tax form instead of the lengthier Form 1040—by using the standard deduction to get to AGI. The standard deduction typically rises a bit each year because it is one of the many items in the tax code pegged to inflation. For the 2003 tax year, the return filed in April 2004, the standard deduction is $4,750 for a single taxpayer and $9,500 for a married couple filing jointly. Once you hit age 65, your standard deduction rises by $950; a married couple where both are 65 or over have a standard deduction of $11,400. If you are legally blind, add in another $950.

You may also take some "above-the-line" deductions even if you do not itemize deductions. These deductions reduce the amount of income subject to tax and may be claimed for

- contributions to an Individual Retirement Account for eligible taxpayers, up to $3,000 a year or $3,500 a year for those age 50 and over
- interest on qualified student loans, up to $2,500, for those meeting income requirements
- out-of-pocket expenditures by teachers for classroom supplies up to $250
- expenses of a job-related move where your new workplace is at least fifty miles farther away from your old home than your previous workplace

- one half of self-employment (Social Security) taxes and, as of 2003, every penny you pay toward health insurance premiums if you are self-employed

## Itemized Deductions

If your allowable deductions exceed the standard amount and will produce a lower tax bill, you may itemize individual deductions using Schedule A attached to Form 1040. Being too lazy to do the arithmetic can cost you money. If you paid $8,000 in mortgage interest, $3,000 in combined state and local income taxes, and gave $2,000 to charity, for a total deductible amount of $13,000, you'll clearly come out ahead by itemizing instead of taking the standard married couple deduction of $9,500. Yet, according to the U.S. Congress General Accounting Office, *more than 500,000 taxpayers overpaid their taxes* in recent years because they failed to itemize—even though their mortgage payments alone exceeded their standard deductions. On average, each of these taxpayers paid over $600 more than necessary.

## Action Plan

**Step One:** Add up all your deductible expenses for the year.

**Step Two:** Determine whether your tax bill will be lower by taking the standard deduction or by itemizing.

**Step Three:** Whether you take the standard deduction or itemize deductions, be sure to claim eligible above-the-line deductions.

## Deduction Categories

There are four principal categories of itemized deductions: charitable contributions, interest, taxes, and unreimbursed medical expenses.

- Deductible contributions are those made to qualified charities (see Chapter 12).
- Interest deductions consist primarily of mortgage interest (see Chapter 7).
- State and local income taxes along with real estate and personal property taxes are all deductible on your federal income tax return.
- Out-of-pocket medical expenses are also deductible, but only to the extent that they exceed 7.5 percent of adjusted gross income (see Chapter 11).

There is also a fifth grouping of "miscellaneous itemized deductions," deductible only to the extent that their total exceeds 2 percent of adjusted gross income. This category includes such items as

- job-hunting expenses
- safe-deposit rental
- tax preparation costs
- legal fees related to producing taxable income or obtaining tax advice
- IRA fees paid directly and not out of the account
- dues to unions or professional organizations

**Tax tip:** Although most tax-related expenditures are deductible under the "miscellaneous itemized deductions" category, don't try to claim the fees imposed by a credit card company for paying your tax bill via the card—the IRS has explicitly said that this is a nondeductible personal expense.

Whether to claim the standard deduction or itemized deductions may depend more on your lifestyle than your income. In other words, it's wrong to assume that middle-class taxpayers should always take the standard deduction, while only the wealthy can itemize deductions. You may be firmly in the middle class—but if you own a mortgaged home and live in a high-tax state, you're probably better off itemizing. A Vanderbilt living mortgage-free in a no-tax state, on the other hand, may have no reason to itemize deductions.

---

### TAX HAVENS

There are seven states with no state income tax (although they may make up for the lack of income tax by imposing other taxes):
- Alaska
- Florida
- Nevada
- South Dakota
- Texas
- Washington
- Wyoming

---

Pay attention to your personal situation and, if you make lifestyle changes, reevaluate your overall tax planning, including your decision about taking the standard deduction or itemizing deductions. Moving to another state, getting married or divorced, becoming a parent, or buying a house can have a major impact on your tax obligation. Also pay attention—and consult a tax specialist before making any moves—if your income reaches the phaseout level where you will lose some deductions.

## Phasing Out

The Vanderbilts and their friends often lose the benefit of itemized deductions. Two different tax provisions come into play:

1. Most deductions disappear when taxpayers become subject to the alternative minimum tax (AMT), a tax system designed to eliminate loopholes that benefit the rich (for more on the AMT, which is affecting more and more middle-class taxpayers, see Chapter 12).
2. Taxpayers with adjusted gross income of more than $139,500, whether single or married filing jointly for the 2003 tax year, are also subject to phaseouts that limit the value of many itemized deductions. Phaseouts, sneaky little things that creep up throughout the tax code, are Congress's way of boosting revenue—or, put another way, of taking back with one hand the tax breaks that it gives with the other.

The phaseout on deductions works like this: If your income exceeds the threshold, the total of your itemized deductions for taxes, mortgage interest, charitable gifts, job expenses, and most miscellaneous deductions is reduced by 3 percent of the amount by which your AGI exceeds the threshold. You never lose *all* your deductions, if that's any consolation, because (1) deductions for medical expenses, casualty and theft losses, investment interest expense, and gambling losses are not affected by phaseouts, and (2) you can never lose more than 80 percent of the affected deductions. If John and Mary have an AGI of $300,000, with otherwise deductible expenses of $50,000, they lose $4,815 of their deductions ($300,000 minus $139,500 × 3 percent). Instead of $50,000 in itemized deductions, they may deduct $45,185.

## DON'T MISS OUT!

Some deductions are obvious. Others may slip beneath your radar screen. Here are a few you might overlook:
- contact lenses, eyeglasses, and hearing aids
- cellular phones used for business
- gambling losses to the extent of gambling gains
- long-term-care insurance premiums
- points on a home mortgage
- state personal property taxes on cars and boats

## Deductions by the Bunch

If your itemized deductions total just a bit more than the standard deduction, you can take advantage of a strategy called "bunching" to maximize tax savings. Bunching simply means itemizing deductions every other year, grouping them in those years for maximum benefit while taking the standard deduction in alternate years.

Bunching works best if your average deductions are close to your standard deduction. It won't work unless the standard deduction will exceed itemized deductions in alternate (nonbunching) years. And it won't work if your income is so high—more than $139,500 in 2003 and estimated (at this writing) to be $142,700 in 2004—that you start to lose the benefit of itemized deductions. For more on timing strategies, including bunching, see Chapter 12.

## Action Plan

If bunching deductions in alternate years will be beneficial, take these steps:

**Step One:** If you typically make most of your charitable contributions each December, wait until January in bunching years, then make them again that December—doubling deductions for the year—and skip the following year.

**Step Two:** Assuming that you usually visit the dentist twice a year, schedule checkups in January, June, and December in bunching years; then make a single visit in June of the following year.

**Step Three:** Schedule elective medical procedures in alternate years. An emergency appendectomy can't wait, but a tummy tuck can be accelerated or postponed.

**Step Four:** Prepay January mortgage interest in December in alternate years.

**Step Five:** Pay first-quarter property taxes in December in alternate years.

## AVERAGE ITEMIZED DEDUCTIONS

| Adjusted Gross Income | Contributions | Interest | Taxes | Medical Expenses |
|---|---|---|---|---|
| $20,000–$30,000 | $1,700 | $6,317 | $2,297 | $5,815 |
| $30,000–$50,000 | 1,829 | 6,595 | 3,093 | 5,038 |
| $50,000–$75,000 | 2,123 | 7,406 | 4,324 | 5,565 |
| $75,000–$100,000 | 2,604 | 8,578 | 5,896 | 7,364 |

| AVERAGE ITEMIZED DEDUCTIONS | | | | *(continued)* |
|---|---|---|---|---|
| Adjusted Gross Income | Contributions | Interest | Taxes | Medical Expenses |
| $100,000–$200,000 | 3,733 | 11,310 | 9,239 | 11,226 |
| $200,000+ | 21,301 | 26,144 | 39,691 | 31,470 |

Averages are for information only; your own deductions must be substantiated with proper documentation.

© 2003, CCH Incorporated. All Rights Reserved. Reprinted with permission.

# Credits

Other savings come from credits built into the tax code. Credits are actually worth more than deductions. Tax deductions reduce the amount of your taxable income, so the dollars you save depend on your tax bracket. If you are in the 31-percent tax bracket, a deduction saves you 31 cents on the dollar, or $31 on $100 of expenditure. In contrast, tax credits are a dollar-for-dollar reduction in the amount of tax you owe. A tax credit of $100 saves you $100.

Tax credits include the following:

- A child tax credit of $1,000 is available for each dependent under age 17 at the close of the tax year, phasing out for taxpayers with modified adjusted gross income of $75,000 for single taxpayers and $110,000 for married taxpayers filing jointly. Unless extended by Congress, the credit will fall back to $700 in 2005.
- A child and dependent care credit helps two-income working couples with the costs—up to $3,000 a year for one child, up to $6,000 for two or more—of day care, a

baby-sitter, and school tuition. For taxpayers with an AGI of over $15,000, the credit is a maximum of 35 percent of the qualifying amount, or a maximum of $1,050 for one child, $2,100 for two or more. The credit is reduced as the AGI goes up so that taxpayers with an AGI of over $43,000 qualify for a maximum of 20 percent of the qualifying amount ($600 for one child, $1,200 for two or more).

- An adoption credit of up to $10,160 for the actual expenses involved in an adoption, the full $10,160 (regardless of how much is spent) if the child has special needs, reduced at AGI of $152,390 and ending at $192,390.
- The Hope scholarship credit provides a maximum allowable credit of $1,500 per student for tuition paid in each of the first two years of postsecondary education.
- The Lifetime Learning credit provides a per-family credit of 20 percent of tuition expenses up to $10,000 per year. Both education credits completely phase out for single taxpayers at AGI of $51,000 and for married taxpayers filing jointly at $103,000.

## Get Organized

Now that you understand tax basics, you can start to get organized. There are three important steps to take:

1. First, if you haven't already done so, organize last year's tax receipts by category.
2. At the same time, start a file for this year's tax receipts, to keep as you go along.
3. Think long-term and organize important papers that will be needed for future tax returns.

Some people get a kick out of organizing files—I recently read a newspaper column by a woman who remembered an accordion file as a favorite childhood Christmas gift. Many more people probably find the job tedious. But putting your papers in order puts you on the road to good financial management—and much easier tax preparation.

Perhaps you're a paperless person. If you use money-management software to manage your finances, your expenses will be automatically grouped by category as you move through the year. If you then use tax-preparation software to prepare your tax return, the information can easily transfer from one software program to the other.

You can also use software to store documents or to organize paper documents. If you want to do away with paper altogether (a course that makes me nervous, unless you diligently back up your computer files), you can scan important documents into your PC or Mac and store them in digital form. If you choose to keep your paper documents, you may find a software-based inventory system to be helpful. Either way, be sure to keep a backup disk in a secure location away from home. And think in terms of organizing last year's files, getting started on organizing this year's tax documents, and thinking long-term.

## Action Plan

### Step One: Organize Last Year's Tax Receipts

If your tax receipts are currently floating in various locations around your home and office—in your desk, a bureau drawer, some perhaps still in your wallet—the first step is gathering them all in one place.

1. Buy file folders or an accordion file and label each folder or section by tax-related categories: medical expenses, charitable donations, taxes (state and local income tax, property tax), and investments (purchases and sales). If you are

## Action Plan

### Step One: Organize Last Year's Tax Receipts

self-employed, label a file for business expenses (see Chapter 7 for more details). File receipts and canceled checks by category.

2. Start a separate file for receipts for non–tax related items—such as credit card bills for shoes or a toaster—that need be kept only until the next statement records the payment or, in the case of a warranty item such as an appliance, until the warranty expires.

Tackling every one of these tasks—this month, without delay—will make your life much easier when tax filing time rolls around in April. Following the simple steps in this chapter will make it easy to get started.

Okay. Relax. Take a break. That's enough effort for now. The next step will be easier because you can apply the lessons learned in organizing last year's records.

## Action Plan

### Step Two: Organize This Year's Tax Receipts

You'll find it much easier to keep records as you go along—and much easier to prepare next year's tax return when the time comes. Again, you can save both time and money by following these simple steps:

1. Start a file for the current year, labeling by tax-related categories. These file folders are the place to keep receipts and

## Action Plan

### Step Two: Organize This Year's Tax Receipts

documents supporting charitable contributions, unreimbursed business expenses, investment gains and losses, and, if you are self-employed, home office expenses.

2. Prepare a summary sheet for each deductible category as you file your receipts and canceled checks. Such a summary will be enormously helpful in preparing your tax return, whether you do it yourself or turn it over to a professional. Do it yourself and you'll save money, use a professional preparer (see Chapter 2) and you'll save time. For the summary, use a notebook such as the ruled accountants' ledgers available in any stationery shop and label each column by deduction category. Then, in the column headed *Medical,* enter, by date, every doctor and dental visit, pair of eyeglasses, and prescription medication. At tax time you can quickly add up the column and see if your medical expenses exceed the 7.5 percent of AGI necessary to claim a deduction.

3. As you balance your checkbook each month, separate the canceled checks and file them by tax category. Use a separate file for receipts and canceled checks that have nothing to do with taxes. This will save lots of time at year-end, when you can toss the run-of-the-mill canceled checks—for your haircuts or your hiking boots—and save the tax-related items for the period of time that your return may be subject to audit (see Chapter 10).

Time for another break. Catch your breath, then put the lessons you've learned about organizing past and current tax files to good use in preparing for the future.

## Action Plan

Step Three: Think Long-term

1. Keep canceled checks and receipts substantiating tax returns for a minimum of four years—three years after the date of filing (April 2007 for the return filed in 2004 for the 2003 tax year).
2. Keep records on property subject to capital-gains tax—such as investments and your home—for four years beyond the date they are sold. You will need information on their cost basis (the original purchase price plus expenses associated with the purchase) in order to calculate the gain and any tax due on the gain. (See Chapter 7 for more details on the sale of real estate, Chapter 9 on investments.)
3. Keep records relating to retirement plan contributions and distributions almost indefinitely to help you meet stringent IRS requirements about amounts and timing (see Chapters 4 and 6). If you have had a nondeductible IRA along with deductible plans, you must file a Form 8606 reporting form each year—and keep those forms, along with each year's Form 1040—to prove that distributions from the nondeductible IRA are not taxable.

## MOVING ON

When you move and send change-of-address notices to your nearest and dearest, be sure to notify the IRS by sending Form 8822 to the address where you filed your last return. Instead, if

## MOVING ON

you wish, you may send a signed letter giving your old and new addresses along with your full name and Social Security or tax identification number. The IRS uses the address on your most recent tax return when it sends notices concerning audits and other matters. Not receiving such notices is no excuse for non-compliance.

## Today's To-do List

There are two more items on the list of things to do this month: Adjust your on-the-job withholding to accurately reflect your tax liability, and prepare tax forms for household help.

### Adjust Withholding

The withholding system is designed so that, properly used, you come out even—at the end of the year, you don't owe Uncle Sam anything and he doesn't owe you anything. On income where tax is not withheld—investment income, for example, or Social Security retirement benefits—quarterly estimated income tax installments are also meant to have you come out even. If the balance must tip one way or the other, you're better off *paying* a modest amount when you file your return.

Yet many taxpayers think refunds are the way to go. For one recent tax year, the IRS reported that it had received 128 million individual tax returns—and it had issued *91 million refunds.*

Don't fall into the refund trap. You may view refunds as a form of forced saving. But there are better ways to save, even when interest rates are low. If you receive a refund, you have earned nothing on your money for months on end. In effect, you've made an interest-free loan to Uncle Sam and temporarily lost the use of the money. Keep this in mind—and adjust your withholding, if you haven't already done so, to reflect the lower tax rates enacted in 2003 as well as the personal exemptions and deductions you take when you fill out your federal income-tax return.

The more allowances you claim on the W-4, the less income tax is withheld. To a certain extent, you can tinker with the allowances to boost your cash flow. With three kids and a stay-at-home spouse, you would normally be entitled to five allowances. If you will be adding to your family this year, through birth or adoption, you can add an extra allowance to reflect the new dependency exemption. If the Hope scholarship credit will reduce your taxable income, you can add an allowance to reduce withholding. Or, if you anticipate a tax windfall in the form of large deductions—perhaps you started contributing to a retirement plan or your home was hit by a hurricane and you suffered a casualty loss—you could take more allowances. But be careful. If you claim withholding allowances that reduce the amount of tax withheld, and can't justify the claim as being reasonable, the IRS will slap you with a $500 penalty. Taxpayers are generally allowed up to ten withholding allowances without challenge. More than that and you'd best have a reasonable explanation.

If you wind up underwithheld—perhaps because you sold stock at a substantial gain near year-end or lost a mortgage interest deduction when you moved from a house to a rental apartment—you can make up the difference by having additional amounts withheld from your remaining paychecks during the year. Alternatively, you can make an estimated tax payment by January 15 of the year in which you will file the return for the preceding year. Be sure to do one or the other or you will wind up with a penalty.

If you do have a refund coming this year, you may want to have it applied to next year's tax bill. Then you can decrease your withholding and put more money in your pocket in the course of the year. Alternatively, take the money and put it to work in a tax-advantaged retirement plan.

## Pay Taxes for Household Help

If you employ household help on a regular basis and pay that person more than $1,300 in a calendar year, you must give the worker a W-2 form by the end of January and file a W-3 form with the Social Security Administration by the end of February. The tax itself is reported and paid on Schedule H attached to your federal income-tax return.

The rule applies to cleaning help, gardeners, and baby-sitters—any regular help that works for you and not an independent third-party employer. If you pay a lawn service to mow your lawn each week, you are not required to give W-2 forms to the guys who run the mowers. If you personally hire a nanny to care for your preschool children, however, you are obligated to file these forms. And if you pay that employee more than $1,000 in any calendar quarter, you are also required to withhold income tax and pay the federal unemployment tax.

Observance of this law is spotty at best—it picked up after Zoe Baird lost out on becoming President Bill Clinton's attorney general because she failed to pay Social Security taxes for her nanny—but has fallen off in recent years. Maybe people no longer want to be attorney general. But the law is the law. If you are required to pay these taxes, you should do so. Granted, many occasional workers prefer to be paid in cash and don't really want you to report their income. If you go along, you may eventually get into trouble—whether or not you wish to hold high government office. One New Yorker faced an expensive tax bill in the form of back tax plus interest and penalties when her weekly housecleaner retired and decided she wanted Social Security retirement benefits.

## TAX TIPS FOR JANUARY

- **Avoid penalties** and interest by filing and paying taxes on time
- **Pay fourth-quarter estimates** by January 15
- **Adjust withholding if** necessary to reflect new lower tax rates
- **Determine whether to claim the standard deduction** or itemize deductions
- **Organize tax records** and save both time and money

# CHAPTER 2

# February
## Finding Help

As the tax laws become increasingly complicated with each passing year, you may give in and join the hordes of people who seek help in preparing their income-tax returns.

If your financial life is reasonably straightforward, you should be able to tackle your own returns. This is especially true if you typically file the short versions of federal income-tax returns, Form 1040EZ or Form 1040A (see Chapter 3 for more information on these simple tax return forms). Even if you typically itemize deductions and file Form 1040, tax preparation software makes it easy for most folks to do their own—just plug in the numbers. If you use record-keeping software all year, as discussed in Chapter 1, it will be even easier—most of the relevant numbers will be in place before you begin.

Choosing tax-preparation software is also relatively straightforward. The two major software programs are H&R Block's TaxCut and Intuit's TurboTax; both let you enter all the data on your computer, then file electronically or print a tax form to file by mail. Both have useful help functions within the software and, at an additional cost, a feature allowing you to e-mail a question to an expert and get an answer.

But if your life was at all complicated in the last tax year—you went through a divorce, had business income, bought rental property, assumed the care of elderly parents, came into an inheritance—you may want to consult a professional for help in preparing your tax return. (In fact, if you prepare your return yourself, you may want to ask a professional to review it to make sure you haven't overlooked some critical detail. Review won't cost as much as full-scale tax preparation and it can ensure peace of mind.)

## BEYOND TAX PREP

You may also want to rely on a tax professional for year-round advice, getting in touch before making a major financial move. Doing so would have saved megabucks for one wealthy individual. When he sold his business, he made a $500,000 charitable contribution to reduce his tax bite in a year with multimillion-dollar income from the sale. But he failed to ask his accountant before making the contribution and learned—after the fact—that in his tax bracket only 20 percent of the contribution could be deducted. The rest certainly benefited the charity but was of no help to the bottom line on his tax return. How could it happen? As his accountant could have told him, there is a hidden tax on high-bracket taxpayers; they begin to lose the benefit of itemized deductions when adjusted gross income exceeds certain limits. This is the phaseout on deductions discussed in Chapter 1.

You may not make a $500,000 contribution (although it would be nice if you could). You may not fall victim to the phaseout on itemized deductions or the dreaded alternative minimum tax, but you could make a costly mistake if you act before asking. As an example, you might want to put $11,000 in a grandchild's college fund, because this is the maximum tax-free gift that can be made in any one year. That's fine—just don't give that same grandchild a birthday check in the same year.

One tip: For personal service on an individual income-tax return, you probably do not want a supersized firm; you may get lost in the shuffle. On the other hand, while many competent and knowledgeable practitioners go solo, you may be better off with a group. At the very least, be sure a sole practitioner has contingency plans in place in case the flu bug bites or a family emergency demands time that should be going to your tax return.

## Picking a Pro

The single most important thing to look for in a tax preparer is familiarity with our ever-changing tax laws and regulations. Between 1995 and 2003 there were almost 1,500 changes in tax law, some of them—the 2003 tax act is a good example—of significant complexity. Not only are new laws complex; many have retroactive effective dates. Worse, more and more seem to have effective dates pegged to a future year. The planned repeal of the federal estate tax in 2010 has generated lots of publicity; the loss of the deduction for college tuition in 2006 may catch many parents unprepared. Someone who occasionally does tax returns for relatives and friends may not be tracking all of these developments and may overlook changes that could save (or cost) you money.

Anyone can hang out a shingle as a tax preparer. There are no national standards or licensing exams for tax practitioners, although some must meet professional requirements (see below), so you're on your own in making a choice. It isn't easy. Professional help comes in several guises and at varying costs. It can be expensive—although the fees you pay for tax preparation may be included in miscellaneous itemized deductions (if you itemize deductions) on Schedule A attached to Form 1040. Miscellaneous deductions, as a group, are deductible to the extent that they exceed 2 percent of adjusted gross income.

**Commercial preparers,** both local practitioners and the national franchise firms such as the ubiquitous H&R Block, are available at tax time but may or may not be available year-round should you have a question or—worse—receive an audit notice. In general, these firms can save you time but shouldn't be relied on for sophisticated advice to meet complicated situations. Bear in mind that many of their employees are seasonal part-time workers who have attended a tax preparation seminar but who may not have had much practical experience.

**Enrolled agents** are certified by the IRS after having worked for the IRS for at least five years or passing a government exam. They are experienced tax specialists, authorized to represent you before the IRS if you are audited. A referral service is available through the National Association of Enrolled Agents, toll-free at 1-800-424-4339.

**Certified public accountants** have met educational requirements and passed professional qualifying exams in the state where they practice. Those who work in the tax arena can represent clients before the IRS and can provide year-round tax planning advice. Some CPAs have also taken additional training so that they can provide assistance with all aspects of personal financial planning. If you want this additional expertise, look for the designation PFPS (Personal Financial Planning Specialist) or CFP (Certified Financial Planner) in addition to the CPA. Your state organization of CPAs may provide a free referral service to help you find a CPA in your area.

**Tax attorneys,** possibly the tax specialists with the highest fees, specialize in complex tax planning and preparation for individuals and business entities. You probably don't need the services of a tax attorney unless you have high net worth and technical questions concerning, for example, a strategy to shelter income from taxation or a trust to preserve assets for your grandchildren.

## The Interview

Your situation is unique, and you may have any number of questions to pose to potential tax preparers, but here are some you definitely should ask.

- What are your professional qualifications?
- Do you belong to any professional associations?
- How do you keep up-to-date with changing tax laws and regulations?
- Do you prepare returns for people like me, with similar occupations, income levels, investments, or tax issues?
- What information do you need to prepare my return and how would you like it submitted?
- Do you rely on computer software to prepare tax returns?
- Do you have specialists to call on when necessary?
- Will anyone else in your office review my return for accuracy and for interpretations of tax regulations?
- Will you tell me if anything on my return is likely to be challenged by the IRS or state tax authorities?
- Will you watch for, and tell me, if I am missing any opportunities to reduce the tax I owe?
- Will you represent me in an audit?
- Can you give me names of clients as references?
- How much will it cost to prepare my tax return?

## Style Counts

Another good area to explore before hiring a tax preparer is his or her professional style. Some advisers are aggressive in the tax positions they take—and some clients want them to be. Others, boasting that their clients are never audited, may be too conservative, failing to take legitimate deductions if they suspect those deductions might tempt an audit. The tax code contains many gray areas, where you may or may not want to push the limits. The important thing is not how aggressive the preparer is but whether the level of risk-taking matches yours.

For most people, a middle road is best. There's little point in relinquishing legitimate deductions because of suspicion that they may provoke an IRS audit—if you're entitled to a home-office deduction, you should claim it (see Chapter 7)—but you may not want to test the limits of IRS patience either. Ask whether the practitioner's returns are frequently audited, whether he or she challenges the IRS on specific issues, and what is the typical outcome of client audits (many audits actually result in refunds)—and then decide on your comfort level. There's nothing wrong, by the way, with returns being subject to audit. A practitioner who is so conservative that no return is ever audited is probably missing some legitimate tax savings for clients.

## Action Plan

To choose a tax preparer:

**Step One:** Ask family, friends, and—better yet—other professional advisers for their recommendations. A financial planner or attorney may be better able to assess a tax preparer's professional competence than a well-meaning relative or friend.

**Step Two:** Call two or three recommended tax practitioners and interview them, being sure to ask the questions on page 29.

**Step Three:** This month, meet with your chosen tax preparer. You shortchange yourself if you wait until late March or early April, when tax practitioners are very busy and have less time to devote to your return. Delay also gives you less time to round up any documents that may be missing. Procrastination raises the cost of tax preparation along with your blood pressure.

## Preparing for Your Meeting

The cost of preparing a federal tax return can range from less than $100 to many thousands of dollars, depending on the type of tax preparer you use and—more important—the complexity of your affairs and the level of your preparation. You can reduce the cost by getting your documents together and providing your tax adviser with the necessary information in an organized manner. You don't really want to pay a professional's hourly rate to sort through a shoebox full of tax receipts.

### Action Plan

To keep tax-preparation costs down:

**Step One:** If you haven't done so on an ongoing basis (see Chapter 1), prepare summaries of your tax-related information, including deductible mortgage interest and charitable contributions. Give your tax preparer the summaries, keeping the backup documents in case they are needed. If you give your accountant every scrap of paper, he or she will feel obligated to review it all—and the costs will mount accordingly.

**Step Two:** If your tax adviser provides an annual tax organizer or questionnaire for your use in summarizing the relevant information, use it. Filling in the organizer will help you cover all the bases, possibly saving money and avoiding tax penalties.

**Step Three:** Match your records with all the 1099 information returns summarizing income you received in the form of dividends, interest, and other miscellaneous income such as consulting fees and royalties. The IRS matching program will pick up any discrepancies, so—believe me—it's best to avoid

## Action Plan

them. Review these forms as they come in and, if you find something that doesn't match your own records, ask the issuer for a corrected 1099 form.

**Step Four:** Review your tax return from the previous year and provide a copy to your tax preparer if you've hired someone new. If there have been no major changes in your personal or economic circumstances, last year's return will be a good guide to the current year. If there have been significant changes, a review will help you identify areas of possible concern. It will also help pinpoint pertinent information that may reduce this year's taxes. An example might be investment losses that can be carried forward from year to year, offsetting first investment gains and then ordinary income (see Chapter 11). Another example is points on a mortgage refinancing (see Chapter 6).

## ON-LINE TAX HELP

Answers to tax questions may be found on these Web sites:
- **www.irs.gov** is the official IRS site, offering tax forms and publications
- **www.taxsites.com/state.html** for information from state and local tax authorities
- **www.taxweb.com** has links to a range of tax resources
- **www.nolo.com** is a site run by self-help publishers Nolo Press

## Consumer Beware

I can't repeat this warning too often: Anyone—you, your Uncle Harry, your friendly neighbor, a retiree hired by a store-front tax-preparation service, an accountant—can fill out a tax return. There are no national licensing requirements, although some tax practitioners—such as enrolled agents and CPAs—have met professional qualifications.

Unfortunately, as in any field, there are good apples and bad ones. There are incompetent tax preparers out there—and using one can have serious consequences. Some taxpayers underpay their taxes and end up paying hefty amounts in interest and penalties. Others pay more tax than necessary. The U.S. General Accounting Office recently estimated that more than two million taxpayers overpaid their 1998 taxes by $945 million because they claimed the standard deduction when it would have been more beneficial to itemize. Half of these taxpayers used a paid preparer. The GAO said taxpayers likely contributed to some of the errors, but the findings raise questions about the extent of errors caused by paid preparers. Or, as Senator Chuck Grassley, chairman of the Committee on Finance, commented in reporting the GAO findings, "It's counterintuitive that professionals actually could make us worse off."

Some preparers are just lazy and/or careless. When a CPA transposed digits in my husband's Social Security number, the State of New Jersey decided we hadn't paid quarterly estimates. It took years to set the matter straight. And, unfortunately, there are some downright dishonest tax preparers. Run, don't walk, from any tax adviser who suggests that you "forget" unreported income or go into a tax "shelter" with overvalued assets and no income. The IRS has been conducting a decades-long campaign against "abusive" tax shelters and trusts (see Chapter 10); you don't want to be caught in the cross fire. Moreover, your chances of audit actually increase if you use a preparer the IRS has reason to think is incompetent or dishonest.

## CRIMINAL CHARGES

In 2003, the IRS more than doubled the number of criminal investigations of unscrupulous tax preparers. Fraudulent practices often involve claims for inflated personal or business expenses, false deductions, or excessive exemptions. The practitioners benefit by charging inflated fees, guaranteeing large refunds, and diverting a portion of any refund to their own accounts. Warning signs that a practitioner may be dishonest include:

- **Claims that they can obtain larger refunds** than other preparers
- **Fees based on a percentage** of the amount of the refund
- **Refusal to sign** the tax return, including the preparer's federal identification number, or provide the taxpayer with a copy of the return for their records

No matter who prepares it, you are legally responsible for your tax return. The burden of accuracy is on you. Be sure to carefully review your return and make sure it's correct before you sign on the dotted line. If the return is finished too close to April 15, get an extension (see pages 53–54) rather than filing it without adequate review. Ask questions if there is *anything* you don't completely understand. And get a copy of the return for your records.

## Warning Signs

It isn't easy to find out whether a tax preparer is likely to be trouble. The professional associations don't readily reveal disciplinary information. Your state board of accountancy may tell you if a CPA is licensed and if there are any disciplinary actions outstanding. You can also ask a preparer, in your initial meeting, whether his or her license is current and whether any complaints have ever been filed.

One red flag: Watch out for practitioners who also peddle investment products or who receive commissions for referring clients to others—even though these actions may not be illegal or unethical. Commissions for accountants used to be prohibited by state law, but most states have changed those laws. Commissions also used to be considered unethical, but the American Institute of Certified Public Accountants, the standard-setting body for the profession, reversed its anticommission position in 1991 in an effort to help accountants remain competitive with other financial advisers. But—and it's a very big *but* in my mind—while your accountant may indeed be able to recommend suitable investments because he or she knows you and your financial affairs so well, what you want above all in an adviser is objectivity. You want advice that is tailored to you without regard to financial incentives for the adviser. So be careful of potential conflicts of interest as you choose accountants, financial planners, and other advisers.

## KEEPING SECRETS

Once you share information with a tax preparer authorized to practice before the IRS, don't expect that preparer to keep it secret. Although the attorney-client privilege was extended to nonattorneys in a 1998 IRS restructuring, the privilege does not extend to tax returns. According to Mark Luscombe, principal federal tax analyst with CCH, "Communications with respect to tax return preparation are not protected under the law, and taxpayers should not make the mistake of assuming that everything told to accountants is considered privileged communication."

## Help from the IRS

The IRS would like you to think that it is a taxpayer-friendly source of information and help. It urges taxpayers to get in touch via a Web site (www.irs.gov) and toll-free telephone numbers. Tax forms and publications can be ordered by calling 1-800-829-3676. Prerecorded messages on various tax topics can be heard at 1-800-829-4477. Individual questions can be posed by calling 1-800-829-1040.

The IRS Web site does have fact sheets to lend guidance on specific topics. For individual questions, however, you need to speak with a human being. With increasing reliance by the IRS on computerized call centers and automated voice-mail systems, this is not an easy task. Even tax professionals are finding the system hard to navigate. And the IRS Taxpayer Advocate, Nina Olson, was quoted in 2003 as saying that a reorganization of the IRS has "hurt customer service, absolutely."

If you can't get through on the telephone, or prefer face-to-face conversation, the IRS also offers in-person help at its local offices. You can walk in, or you can call to schedule an appointment by leaving a message for Everyday Tax Solutions assistance. The IRS promises a callback within two business days to schedule an in-person appointment at your convenience.

Unfortunately, even when answers are forthcoming, it is often a case of taxpayer beware. There are many gray areas in the tax code and its implementing IRS regulations, so that different interpretations may be provided in answer to the same question. Worse, the courts have said that you can't rely on IRS-supplied information, in most instances, to support a position you take on your tax return. It is helpful, however, if you can secure an answer from the IRS in writing. Always remember, though, that you tend to get what you pay for. IRS advice is free. With complex questions, it is definitely worthwhile to pay for professional advice.

## TAX TIPS FOR FEBRUARY

- **If you do your own taxes**, tax preparation software may be helpful.
- **Consult a tax professional** if your affairs are complicated or if you want to do long-range tax planning.
- **In picking a professional,** get referrals and ask probing questions.

## CHAPTER 3

# March
# Rules of the Road

April 15 is the red-letter day—red as in stop, sit up, and pay attention—when it comes to taxes. But waiting for April to get started is a big mistake. Right now, in March, shed your procrastinating ways and start to think tax. It's the only way to get ahead of the game and to save money, both on tax-preparation fees and on the taxes themselves. You'll save on fees by getting organized. You'll have time to identify tax-saving strategies. And you'll avoid interest and penalties by filing on time.

If your income exceeds specified amounts, you must file a tax return even if you do not owe any money to the IRS. For the 2003 tax year (returns filed in 2004), the filing level is $7,800 for single taxpayers and $14,050 for married taxpayers filing jointly. Where both spouses are 65 or older, and filing jointly, the filing threshold is $15,950. These numbers, like many others in the tax code, are adjusted each year.

If you have net self-employment income of $400 or more, you are also required to file a federal income tax return. This threshold is not adjusted for inflation and hasn't changed in years.

In addition, you must file a return even below these filing thresholds if you are owed a refund. In early 2003, more than

$2.5 billion in refunds was waiting for 1.9 million people who never filed a federal income tax return for 1999. There is a three-year window for claiming a refund, starting with the date the return was due; that gave these careless folks until April 15, 2003, to collect. If you are owed a refund for the 2000 tax year, you have until April 15, 2004, to collect. Miss the date and the refund is lost and gone forever.

## State Income Tax

If your state has an income tax, as most do, you must file your state return at the same time as you file your federal return. Most states—but not all—piggyback on the federal tax structure. This makes life easier because deductions carry over from one tax form to the other.

For residents of some states, however, the state tax form is very different from the federal tax form. Residents of New Jersey, as an example, are allowed very few deductions. On the other hand, they get at least one tax break because uninsured medical expenses, deductible on federal tax returns only to the extent that they exceed 7.5 percent of AGI, are deductible on the New Jersey return once they exceed 2 percent of AGI. This meant that Sherry could see a bit of a silver lining in the $2,500 in dental bills she ran up one year. With an adjusted gross income of $42,000, she could deduct $1,660 ($42,000 × .02 = $840; $2,500 − $840 = $1,660).

Your tax adviser can help you understand what's necessary in your state—and deal with state taxes if you have homes in more than one state—but certain basics apply across the board.

## THE TOLL TAXES TAKE

How much of what you earn goes to paying taxes? Put another way, when does everything you earn finally belong to you? The magic day in 2003—termed "Tax Freedom Day" by the Tax Foundation—was April 19. In 2000, before recent tax cuts by the federal government, it was April 30. In 1913, the year the federal income tax became a permanent fixture, Tax Freedom Day would have arrived on January 30.

## Tax Basics

Getting started on your taxes means deciding which tax forms to use. It means getting a handle on your filing status, exemptions, and tax bracket.

### Tax Forms

Federal tax filing starts with figuring out which form to use. There are three.

*Form 1040EZ* is the simplest form, although—since nothing is easy where the IRS is concerned—it has become more and more complicated in recent years. On the plus side, it can also be used by more taxpayers. You may use the 1040EZ if you

- are filing as single or married filing jointly (not as head of household) and, if filing jointly, are both under age 65
- have taxable income under $50,000 entirely from wages, salaries, tips, taxable grants, unemployment compensation, and interest income of no more than $1,500
- are not claiming any dependents

- are not claiming any credits other than the earned income credit, and
- do not claim any adjustments to income, such as an IRA contribution or student loan interest

You must meet *all* of the above requirements in order to file the 1040EZ. If you do not, but if your income *is* under $50,000, you may be able to file Form 1040A.

To file *Form 1040A*, your income must also be under $50,000. In addition to the above categories, however, income may include dividends, capital-gains distributions, and unemployment compensation. You are allowed to claim adjustments to income for an IRA contribution, a student-loan interest deduction, educator expenses, and a deduction for tuition and fees. You may claim only certain specified credits—such as the child and dependent care credit—and you may not itemize deductions.

All other taxpayers must file the long form, the *Form 1040*, which can be used to report all types of income, deductions, and credits. It is called the long form for good reason, with multiple additional forms, called "schedules," on which to provide details about various transactions. If you will benefit by itemizing deductions, in fact, the 1040 with its accompanying Schedule A is the only form you may use. Schedule B is for listing investment income, all the interest and dividends from bank accounts, stocks, bonds, and mutual funds. Schedule C is used to report self-employment income and offsetting expenses. Schedule D is used to report capital gains and losses during the year. There are additional schedules for other special purposes.

### Filing Status

How will you file? There are five choices: single, married filing jointly, married filing separately, head of household, and widow or widower with a dependent child. For most people this is an easy decision. Single taxpayers do not support other people; heads of household are not currently married but do provide support for at least one other person. For others, filing status may be more complicated.

Married couples generally file as married filing jointly. Indeed, this is usually the most cost-effective way to file, producing the lowest tax bill. If you are married and elect to file as "married filing separately," you'll miss out on many deductions. For example, you cannot claim a deduction for interest on a student loan or a credit for child and dependent care expenses; you cannot take an adoption credit or claim Hope or lifetime learning education credits. Because Uncle Sam wants to discourage married couples from filing separately, you may have to pay more income tax on Social Security retirement benefits. You cannot deduct more than $1,500 in capital losses (instead of $3,000 on a joint return). And you won't be allowed to move money from a traditional IRA into a Roth IRA unless you actually live apart from your spouse for the entire year.

Nonetheless, if you and your spouse both have earned income, you may want to calculate your tax bill both ways—as married filing jointly and as married filing separately—to see which way you come out ahead. That's because the so-called "marriage penalty" (see Chapter 11) pushes the combined income into a higher tax bracket than each would be in if reporting separately. For most people, though, filing separately is a strategy worth considering only if it will lower your tax bill because one of you qualifies for a large deduction subject to limitations. A good example is uninsured medical costs, deductible on the federal return only to the extent that they exceed 7.5 percent of AGI. Let's say Ann and Joe have combined income of $90,000 and Ann had $5,000 in uninsured medical expenses. Since 7.5 percent of $90,000 is $6,750 and Ann's expenses are "only" $5,000, there is no deduction. But if Ann's AGI is $40,000 and she files separately, she can deduct $2,000 (7.5 percent of $40,000 is $3,000, leaving a deduction of the $2,000 balance).

But do this calculation carefully because, as noted above, you lose many tax breaks by filing separately. In addition, tax rates are higher (see table, page 45). Even if it seems to make sense, you would be well advised to consult a tax professional before deciding to file separately while married.

"Qualifying widow or widower" is the last category. You may file a joint return for the year in which your spouse died, even if the death occurred early in the year, so long as you have not remarried. As a surviving spouse, assuming that you were eligible to file a joint return with your spouse in the year of death, you may continue to file as "married filing jointly" for the following two years so long as

- you have not remarried, and
- you paid more than half the cost of maintaining a home in which you cared for a dependent child

## ACCESSORY TO A CRIME?

If you are married but suspect that your spouse is illegally evading taxes, you may not want to sign your name on a joint return. If you file separately, you can avoid liability for the unreported taxes along with interest and penalties.

If you find out after the fact that you signed a return misrepresenting income, you may be able to avoid personal liability by invoking "innocent spouse" rules (see Chapter 11). To succeed, you may have to prove that you were not aware of the misrepresentation. You have two years to claim innocent spouse status, starting with the date the IRS attempts to collect from you. Use Form 8857 to file an innocent spouse election.

## Exemptions

The next step, once you see which tax form to use, is determining the exemptions you may claim. Each personal exemption removes $3,050 from your taxable income for the 2003 tax year; the amount typically goes up each year.

You may claim an exemption for yourself, your spouse (on a joint return), and dependent children. You may also be able to claim exemptions for other dependents, such as your parents (see Chapter 11). As tax publishers CCH Incorporated point out, determining your exemptions isn't quite as easy as counting heads around the family room. All dependents must meet specific eligibility standards. Each dependent must

- be a relative or a member of your household. A baby born on December 31 counts as a dependent for the entire year, as does a child adopted at any time during the year.
- have gross income of under $3,050—except that you may claim children with larger incomes so long as they are under age 19 or full-time students (spending at least five months of the year in school) under age 24
- be a U.S. citizen or national, or a resident of the United States, Canada, or Mexico
- if married, not file a joint return—unless both husband and wife have too little income to be required to file and do so only to receive a refund

In addition to these four tests, you must contribute more than half of the dependent's support for the year. This test must be met even with children who do not have to meet income limitations. In this instance, you may have to demonstrate that their own income was not used for support or that you contributed more toward their support than they did. "Support," in IRS-speak, means expenditures for life's basic necessities—food and lodging, clothing, health care, education, transportation, and recreation. If your child's income is invested, it is not being spent on support. If your child lives at home while commuting to classes, you may calculate the "fair market value" of room and board as part of the support you provide.

Exemptions are phased out for taxpayers with adjusted gross income of $209,250 or more (married filing jointly) or $139,500 (single) for the 2003 tax year; the amounts are indexed annually for inflation. Under the 2001 Tax Act, the phaseout of exemptions will be gradually eliminated between 2006 and 2010. Meanwhile, the phaseout has the direct effect of increasing your marginal tax rate.

## TAX RATES FOR 2003

| Tax Rate | Married Filing Jointly | Single |
|---|---|---|
| 10 percent | $0–$14,000 | $0–$7,000 |
| 15 percent | $14,001–$56,800 | $7,001–$28,400 |
| 25 percent | $56,801–$114,650 | $28,401–$68,800 |
| 28 percent | $114,651–$174,700 | $68,801–$143,500 |
| 33 percent | $174,701–$311,950 | $143,501–$311,950 |
| 35 percent | $311,951 and over | $311,951 and over |
| **Tax Rate** | **Married Filing Separately** | **Head of Household** |
| 10 percent | $0–$7,000 | $0–$10,000 |
| 15 percent | $7,001–$28,400 | $10,001–$38,050 |
| 25 percent | $28,401–$57,350 | $38,051–$98,250 |
| 28 percent | $57,351–$87,350 | $98,251–$159,100 |
| 33 percent | $87,351–$155,975 | $159,101–$311,950 |
| 35 percent | $155,976 and more | $311,951 and more |

## Tax Rates and Brackets

Income-tax rates have gone up and down since the federal income tax became a fixture of American life in 1913. So have the number of tax "brackets," the income range to which each tax rate applies. In the beginning, everyone paid the same percentage of income in tax. At this writing, there are six tax brackets (see table, page 45).

The brackets keep changing because the administration and Congress keep tinkering with the tax code. And they change because they are indexed, automatically adjusted annually to reflect the impact of inflation on income. Indexing keeps you from sliding into a higher tax bracket because you've had a salary increase even when that increase is eroded by rising costs.

Knowing your tax bracket is the key to successful tax planning. Becoming aware of your bracket lets you make the most of deductions. It allows you to plan ahead. As an example, if you expect your tax bracket to be lower next year because you're becoming a one-income couple or taking early retirement, you can shift some deductions into this year when they will be worth more. If possible, you may be able to shift some income into next year, when it will be taxed at a lower rate.

Furthermore, tax attorney Julian Block writes in *Year Round Tax Savings,* "Knowing how much you get to keep after taxes is critical in choosing and implementing all sorts of investment decisions." Bonds producing tax-free income, as an example, are most appropriate for high-bracket taxpayers (see Chapter 9). Gifts of income-producing assets to your children, to shift the tax burden to a lower bracket within the family, also make the most sense for high-bracket taxpayers (see Chapter 12).

## Action Plan

**Step One:** Determine your taxable income by doing the following:

1. Add all income subject to tax—wages, salaries, commissions, tips, dividends, interest, and so on.
2. Subtract deductible IRA contributions, alimony, and (if you are self-employed) one-half of self-employment tax. The result is your adjusted gross income (AGI).
3. Subtract either the standard deduction or itemized deductions, whichever is more. Then subtract personal exemptions of $3,050 for each dependent. The result is your taxable income.

**Step Two:** Look at tax tables to see how much you owe. For 2003, as you can see in the table, an income of $100,000 puts a married couple filing jointly in the 25-percent tax bracket. But that doesn't mean the couple pays $25,000 in federal tax. Some income, such as the $3,050 for each exemption, isn't taxed at all. Then the first $14,000 of income is taxed at 10 percent and the next $42,800 of income at 15 percent. Only the amount over $56,800—and not otherwise reduced by deductions and credits—is taxed at 25 percent. This is the *marginal rate*, the rate on the top dollars subject to tax.

**Step Three:** If you are close to the next marginal bracket, shifting income and deductions may substantially reduce your tax bill. If you expect your tax bracket to be lower next year—perhaps because one of you will stop working temporarily at the birth of a child or because you'll be taking early retirement—you may be able to shift some deductions into this year, when they will be worth more. Or, if possible, you may be able to shift some income into next year, when it will be taxed at a lower rate.

**Step Four:** If you are near or in the top tax bracket, consider moves—such as investing in tax-exempt municipal bonds—to reduce your taxable income.

If you live in a state (and possibly a city) with an income tax, you should calculate your overall tax bracket. If your federal tax bracket is 30 percent and your state income tax is 10 percent, your combined tax rate may appear to be 40 percent. In fact, because the total arrived at by adding the two together is reduced by the federal deduction for the state taxes, your actual combined tax bracket is 37 percent. The deduction is calculated in this example by taking 30 percent of 10 percent, or 3 percent.

## Completing Your Return

Completing a tax return can be a very stop-and-start process, as you make the calculations that must go on various lines of the Form 1040 or its accompanying schedules. You can speed the process—if you're using a pencil-and-paper approach rather than computer software—by using a contemporaneous ledger you've kept throughout the year or by developing a summary worksheet for each category before you begin. Tax-related categories include

- charitable contributions
- state and local income taxes
- real estate and personal property taxes
- unreimbursed medical expenses
- business expenses, if you are self-employed or have unreimbursed employee expenses

To take a simple example, your worksheet for taxes paid during the year might include three subcategories: state and local income taxes, real estate and personal property taxes, and quarterly tax estimates. Go through your checkbook and enter each payment, with date and amount, under the appropriate category on your summary. The bottom line of each ledger page or worksheet will be the number you need for the appropriate line on the tax return. Then, if you haven't yet done so, start keeping an ongoing record for this year's tax payments.

## Filing Your Return

Paper returns should be mailed to the IRS Service Center indicated in your tax packet. The IRS reshuffles the designated centers from time to time, so be sure you send your form to the correct location. Making a mistake will delay your return and could subject you to interest and penalties.

If you are mailing close to the deadline, use "certified mail—return receipt requested" so that you will have proof of timely mailing. A properly dated postmark is supposed to suffice, but a certified mail receipt is surer proof that you met the filing deadline. Or you can shortcut the snail-mail process by sending your return electronically.

---

## Action Plan

**Step One:** Keep an ongoing ledger or summarize checkbook entries at tax-time under tax-related categories.

**Step Two:** Review last year's tax return to be sure you haven't overlooked anything that might reduce this year's taxes, such as

- **investment losses** carried forward from last year (see Chapter 9)
- **points on a refinanced** mortgage. These must be deducted over the life of the mortgage—but if you pay off the mortgage or refinance again, you can deduct the remaining points in the year the mortgage ends.

**Step Three:** When everything is in order—you've double-checked your math, reviewed all your entries, and made sure all necessary forms and schedules are attached—file your return.

## Electronic Filing

The IRS is making an all-out effort to have taxpayers file electronically, holding out the lure of faster refunds. File your tax return electronically and, if you're due a refund, you should receive it twice as quickly than as if you file by regular mail. Authorize automatic deposit of the refund into your bank account, and receipt will be faster still.

Nearly one-third of all individual income tax returns were e-filed in 2000, most of them filed by tax preparers on behalf of their clients. Congress would like to have 80 percent of all tax returns filed electronically by 2007, and the IRS has instituted new programs to encourage more taxpayers to join in the fun.

Here are some options:

- The Free File Alliance is an alliance between the IRS and a group of software companies, offering free on-line tax preparation and electronic filing services to taxpayers who meet specific criteria such as income level. Details are available at www.irs.gov and at www.firstgov.gov.
- The IRS's TeleFile program allows taxpayers to electronically file income tax returns using a touch-tone telephone and a toll-free number. Again, taxpayers must meet specific requirements, including having filed Form 1040EZ the previous year.
- Software programs such as TaxCut and TurboTax let you enter all the data on your computer, then file electronically or print a tax form to file by mail.
- You can prepare your own return and pay a tax preparer to file it for you. Of course, as Kevin Robert of CCH Tax Compliance cautions, you get what you pay for. If you prepare your own return, you can't "expect the firm to be available to respond to IRS inquiries or a potential audit down the road."

- A tax preparer can prepare and e-file your return for you. This gives you the benefit of professional preparation and—if you've chosen the preparer carefully—professional representation should you need it down the road.

Many states are also moving to electronic filing of income tax returns, with forty-two on board at last count. In most instances, you must buy a software program to join in—but in 2003 California was moving toward free on-line filing.

---

### CAUTIONARY NOTE

If you use the IRS Web site to access Free File providers, watch out for sales pitches based on your confidential tax data. In March 2003, several consumer groups warned that some commercial tax preparers participating in the Free File Alliance (1) require taxpayers to waive privacy protection to receive marketing messages from affiliates, and (2) offer nontax products, such as mortgage refinancing, based on personal information entered into the electronic tax form. Indicate that you pay mortgage interest and—despite assurances of privacy from the IRS—you may get a pitch from a mortgage company. Worse, it may be a high-cost mortgage lender.

---

### Collecting from the IRS

The IRS encourages electronic filing, in part, by pointing to faster refunds. It's better to come out even than to receive a refund. However, if you are due a refund:

1. Beware of costly "refund anticipation loans." These loans, secured by the anticipated refund, come at a very

high cost—according to the Consumer Federation of America, annual interest rates range from 67 percent to an astounding 774 percent. You may want to think twice before paying such fees to get your refund a little earlier.
2. Don't ignore tax refunds that might be due. If you think you may be entitled to a refund you haven't received, go to www.irs.gov and follow the directions.

## Penalty Time

What happens if you don't file your return on time? Here's where the biggest price of procrastination comes into play. If you don't get around to filing a federal income-tax return and don't pay anything toward your outstanding tax bill, you will wind up subject to both interest and penalties—and can wind up owing an additional 25 percent of the outstanding balance. If your tax bill was $2,000, that's another $500 in penalties alone!

A recent count reveals more than 150 types of civil penalties in the Internal Revenue Code, for everything from underpaying estimated taxes to taking money out of an Individual Retirement Account before you reach age 59½. However, most civil penalties fall into the following five categories (you can also get socked with criminal penalties—with fines and, if convicted, prison time—for tax evasion, fraudulent returns, or willful failure to file a return at all):

1. **Filing late.** Fail to file your tax return by the final due date, including extensions, and you may be assessed a penalty of 5 percent of the amount due per month, up to a maximum of 25 percent.
2. **Paying late.** Fail to pay tax that is due and you can incur an additional penalty, also to a maximum of 25 percent.
3. **Accuracy.** Understating your income tax liability can lead to a 20 percent penalty.

4. **Filing a "frivolous return."** Protest the income tax by filing an incomplete return or one containing incorrect information and you face a penalty of $500 *in addition to* any other penalties that may apply.
5. **Fraud.** Penalties can reach 75 percent of the amount owed.

In addition to penalties, the IRS levies interest on unpaid bills—compound interest, so that you wind up paying interest on interest until your tax bill is settled to the satisfaction of Uncle Sam. The interest rate changes from time to time. When interest rates are high, the outstanding interest can quickly equal the amount of outstanding tax.

## Payment Options

Don't panic and don't throw in the towel. If you can't get your return in on time, you can get an extension. If you don't have the money to pay your taxes in full and on time, you have additional options. You can arrange payment by credit card, or ask the IRS for an installment agreement.

### Extensions

Securing an extension beyond April 15 is one way to remove some of the springtime pressure—although you must still pay at least 90 percent of your tax liability by April 15 to avoid any penalties. You will also owe interest on the unpaid balance.

Two extensions are available. First, you can delay filing until August 15 via an automatic four-month extension. Secure this extension in one of three ways:

1. file Form 4868 by mail, or
2. send a request electronically via your own tax-preparation software or your tax preparer, or

3. call the IRS, toll-free, at 1-888-796-1074. To make a payment with your request by telephone, you can authorize an electronic withdrawal from your checking or savings account. Have the adjusted gross income from your prior year's tax return on hand and use Form 4868 as a worksheet to prepare for the call. Then enter the confirmation number provided by the IRS on the form and keep it with your tax records.

A second filing extension, until October 15, may be had by filing Form 2688. This one isn't automatic—you must provide reasons for the delay, and the extension is subject to approval by the IRS.

## Extended Payment

Another way to ease the springtime pressure to pay is to pay by credit card. Doing so allows you to spread payment over time. But it's not all gravy. You will pay a percentage of the tax (currently up to 2.49 percent) to the processing company as a "convenience fee," and you will have to pay finance charges and interest imposed by your credit card's issuer. This can be a costly way to defer payment of your tax bill—more costly than you may realize. According to Steve Rhode of Myvesta, a nonprofit consumer education organization, charging a tax bill of $3,000 and paying only the minimum due each month (never a good idea) will cost $7,930 in interest payments over 37 years. The calculation assumes an interest rate of 18 percent and minimum monthly payments of 2 percent.

Alternatively, you may qualify for an installment payment plan. The IRS offers a streamlined approval process if the amount due is not more than $25,000 and you can pay it off within five years. Request an installment plan by attaching Form 9465 (available on the IRS Web site, www.irs.gov) to the front of your tax return, listing the proposed monthly payment amount and the monthly payment date. You may also pay by electronic withdrawal from your checking or savings account.

There is a $43 fee for setting up the installment agreement. You will also pay interest—currently at 5 percent per year, compounded daily—plus a late-payment penalty on the unpaid balance. The late payment penalty, usually 0.5 percent, drops to 0.25 percent when the IRS has approved an installment agreement. So it's clearly better to request an installment agreement than to ignore tax filing altogether. It's also clearly better to pay off as much of your tax bill as possible as quickly as possible.

Sometimes there are good reasons for failure to file on time. If you have a really good reason—if you are seriously ill, for example, or your house burned down—you can request an "abatement" of the penalty. Abatements are sometimes, but not always, granted by the IRS. Don't rely on an abatement. Barring the unforeseen catastrophe, there is no reason to incur a penalty—not if you follow the advice in this book and get organized to pay your taxes on time.

## Estimates

When you file your federal and state income-tax returns for the previous year, don't sit back and relax until you've also paid any first-quarter tax estimates that may be due for the *current* tax year.

Self-employed individuals must file quarterly estimated taxes. For most wage earners, income taxes are collected on a pay-as-you-go basis—in other words, taxes are withheld from your paycheck. But withholding may be insufficient to cover your tax bill if you also have income from interest, dividends, capital gains, rents, or a business. And, if you come up woefully short, owing more than $1,000 after withholding, you will face IRS penalties.

To avoid penalties, make estimated tax payments (by April 15, June 15, September 15, and January 15) based on how much tax you expect to owe. You don't have to calculate your tax bill to the penny—penalties can be avoided if the combination of withholding and estimated tax payments equals at least 90 percent of your tax liability for the current year. If you're not sure how much tax you will owe when the year comes to an end, there's an easy out: Penalties can be avoided by paying 100 percent of your prior year's tax bill—unless you had more than $150,000 in income the year before. In this case, your "safe harbor" to avoid penalties is paying 110 percent of your prior year's tax bill.

But there's a catch that can trap the unwary. Penalties are figured separately for each quarter. Unlike withholding, which can be adjusted midyear, underpaying any single estimated tax installment can produce a penalty even if you overpay a subsequent installment to make up the difference. Penalties can be avoided by using an "annualized" method of computing income and filing Form 2210 with your federal tax return, thereby notifying the IRS that your estimated payments were based on the income actually received in each quarter.

## Fixing Mistakes

If you finish your tax return, heave a sigh of relief, and pop it in the mail (or file electronically) and only then realize you've made a mistake or missed a legitimate deduction, all is not lost. You have three years from the date you file (April 2007 for the return filed in 2004 for the 2003 tax year) to change your return. Do so by filing an amended return on Form 1040X.

Some folks believe that filing an amended return brings you to the attention of the IRS and may result in an audit. Others—and the IRS—deny the assertion. In any event, you will certainly want to file an amended return if it will bring you a tax refund. This could be the case if you overlooked a deduction—or if a deduction became available only after you filed your return. An example of the latter is the IRS ruling freeing home sale gains from tax retroactively if the home was sold prematurely due to death, divorce, or the loss of a job. Another example would be the newly liberalized definition of a home office. And you can file an amended return to backdate a casualty deduction if you live in an area so hard hit by a hurricane, tornado, or other natural disaster that the president declares it an official disaster area. (For more on all of these home-related deductions, see Chapter 7.)

You should also file an amended return if it will undo a mistake. If you overlooked some income, then received a 1099 information return reporting the income, the IRS matching program will pick up the discrepancy; an amended return before the tax deadline can set things right. If you file your tax return early, expecting to receive a refund in time to make the IRA contribution you've claimed as a deduction, then have unexpected expenses eat up the refund, filing an amended return before the official filing date will eliminate the deduction with no harm done.

## TAX TIPS FOR MARCH

- **Tax filing is** easier with Forms 1040EZ and 1040A, if you qualify, but you may save money by itemizing deductions on the long form, 1040.
- **Most married couples** do best by filing jointly, but couples with high medical expenses may benefit by filing as "married filing separately."
- **Tax rates** and brackets keep changing; knowing your marginal rate helps you plan ahead.
- **Electronic filing,** encouraged by the IRS, can speed receipt of refunds.
- **An extension can** let you delay filing your tax return.
- **An amended tax return** may be filed within three years to correct a mistake or an omission.

# SECTION TWO

# Second Quarter: You and Your Job

# CHAPTER 4

# April
# Retirement Plan Tax Savings

One of the best routes to tax savings is putting as much money as possible into tax-sheltered retirement plans such as 401(k) plans and IRAs—and contributing as early in the year as possible. While you are working on last year's taxes is an excellent time—if you haven't done so already—to make your retirement plan contribution for this year.

You may be able to wait until year-end to make your contributions to employer-sponsored retirement plans—more likely you will contribute paycheck by paycheck through automatic deductions. And you can wait right up to tax filing day the following spring to make contributions to Individual Retirement Accounts and retirement accounts for the self-employed. But making your contributions early in the year lets you take full advantage of tax-deferred compounding. Just look at the difference, in an example provided for this book by T. Rowe Price: Both Jessica and Joe contribute the maximum amount permitted each year (see the table on IRA contributions on page 70). Jessica contributes to her IRA on January 1 each year; Joe waits fifteen months longer, putting the money in just before he files his tax return the following April 15. After twenty years, assuming the contributions have earned a steady 8 percent in interest, Jessica has $169,078 and Joe has $153,078. Quite a difference— more than 10 percent—in a retirement nest egg!

## Taxable versus Tax-Deferred

Deciding to contribute—and making every effort to contribute early—is the first step. Deciding where to put your money is just as important. Tax-sheltered retirement plans are not an investment in and of themselves. They are a container in which you place the investments you select. Those investments may be certificates of deposit. They may be mutual funds. They may consist of a mixture of individual stocks for growth and bonds for income.

In an employer-sponsored plan, you will be presented with a menu of investment choices. In an IRA, the choice is practically wide-open (although you can forget about collectibles such as stamps or coins; they are not allowed). In choosing the investment vehicles for your retirement plan, just as you would select any taxable investments you may have, consider your personal goals, time horizon, and attitude toward risk. Then, if you have both tax-deferred retirement accounts and taxable accounts, decide what to put in each account.

Although tax considerations shouldn't *drive* your investment decisions, the 2003 tax changes may influence your thinking with respect to which type of investments belong in tax-deferred accounts and which in taxable accounts. In a tax-deferred account, nothing is taxed until you withdraw your money—but then every penny is taxed at ordinary income rates as high as 35 percent. In a taxable account, interest is taxed each year at ordinary income rates but dividends are now taxed at no more than 15 percent. And capital gains are taxed only when securities are sold, again at a maximum rate of 15 percent. (For more on taxes and investments, see Chapter 9.) With this new tax structure, you may want to hold stocks in your taxable accounts where dividends and any gains will be taxed each year at the new lower rate. Put taxable income-producing bonds in your tax-deferred account, where the interest will not be taxed until withdrawn.

In any case, your tax-sheltered retirement plans should not include either tax-free investments (such as municipal bonds) or tax-deferred investments (such as annuities). Since the plans are themselves tax-sheltered, with no tax on earnings until the money is withdrawn, you gain nothing by including these tax-favored investments; you can't bypass taxes on the same money twice. Indeed, since all distributions from qualified plans are taxed as ordinary income, having tax-free bonds in your retirement plan would actually make you pay taxes on tax-free income!

Tax-deferred retirement savings come in several flavors, including employer-sponsored 401(k) and 403(b) plans, Individual Retirement Accounts, and retirement plans for the self-employed. Contributions, as described below, are often deductible. Earnings are usually tax-deferred until withdrawn.

As if deductible contributions and tax deferral aren't enough, there is another attraction: You may be eligible for a new "saver's credit." Employees and self-employed individuals with income up to $50,000 (for married couples filing jointly) or $25,000 (for single taxpayers) may claim a tax credit ranging from 10 percent to 50 percent for retirement plan contributions. If you pay taxes as a married couple filing jointly and have an adjusted gross income of no more than $30,000, you can claim the maximum 50 percent credit. Since tax credits are dollar-for-dollar savings, a retirement plan contribution of $3,000 actually costs $1,500 out of pocket after a credit of 50 percent is applied. Unless extended by Congress, however, the saver's credit is available only for tax years through 2006.

## Employer-Sponsored Plans

Defined contribution plans such as 401(k) plans in the private sector and 403(b) plans for employees of public schools and tax-exempt organizations allow you to contribute pretax dollars and have them grow, tax-deferred, until they are withdrawn. Pretax means that contributions are deducted from your paycheck and are not part of your taxable income; the contributions do count, however, in calculating your share of the combined Social Security and Medicare (FICA) tax.

In the best plans, an employer match beefs up your contribution. The match may range from as little as 10 cents to more than a dollar for each dollar you contribute, but typically applies to no more than 6 percent of pay. If you are lucky enough to receive an employer match, you should try to contribute at least up to the amount of the match; if you don't, you are throwing away a tax-free boost to your retirement savings. Unfortunately, the recent economic doldrums have led some large corporations to reduce or eliminate their contributions to employee retirement plans. Where matches still exist, they are often limited to employer stock, although you might prefer a broader range of investment options.

Even without an employer match, defined contribution plans have significant advantages:

- Contributions are deducted from your pay, pretax, and are immediately vested. This means that you may take them with you if you leave your job. (Employer contributions, on the other hand, are usually subject to vesting requirements; you must remain in the plan for a specified number of years before you can take this money with you if you leave.)
- Income within the plan—interest, dividends, and capital gains—accumulates tax-deferred.
- And—not least—the contributions reduce your taxable income and therefore your immediate tax liability.

## Your Contributions

The federal government puts a ceiling on how much may be contributed to defined contribution plans. For example, Uncle Sam permits a maximum annual contribution of $13,000 to 401(k) and 403(b) plans in 2004, an amount scheduled to rise for the next few years (see table). You may contribute an additional $3,000 in 2004 if you are age 50 or more, also rising until 2006, after which both regular and catch-up contributions are to be indexed for inflation.

Starting in 2006, employers will be permitted to add a new feature to 401(k) plans, allowing employees to designate some or all of their contributions as Roth contributions. In contrast to most retirement plan contributions, these are after-tax contributions; while they are counted as part of your current taxable income, they are completely tax-free when withdrawn in retirement.

### 401(K) AND 403(B) CONTRIBUTIONS

|  | Maximum Contribution for Workers under Age 50 | Catch-up Contribution for Workers Age 50 and Over |
|---|---|---|
| 2003 | $12,000 | $2,000 |
| 2004 | $13,000 | $3,000 |
| 2005 | $14,000 | $4,000 |
| 2006 and thereafter | $15,000 | $5,000 |

## Investment Choices

A hallmark of defined contribution plans is that you, the employee, decide how to invest the money in the plan. As a result, in direct contrast to the traditional employer-paid pensions that guarantee a specific dollar amount in retirement (now going the way of the dodo), how much you will receive in retirement depends on how much you contribute and how wisely you invest.

When the first 401(k) plans were introduced, in 1981, employees typically had just two investment choices: (1) a guaranteed investment contract, and (2) either company stock or, depending on the particular employer, a growth mutual fund. How times have changed! More than half of all employer-sponsored retirement plans now offer an average of ten mutual funds to employee participants. Many offer employer stock. And a growing number are offering "self-directed plans," where participants may choose among hundreds of mutual funds and almost any individual stock or bond.

More choice isn't always beneficial—especially if it leads you to frequent trades. If you pay commissions or mutual fund fees every time you trade, even in a tax-deferred account, your future retirement nest egg may be a lot smaller than you anticipate.

But don't opt out of choice in favor of employer stock. While you may want to show loyalty to your employer—and growth investments like stock *should* be included in your portfolio—investing too heavily in stock issued by your employer puts both your current income and your future retirement income in the lap of a single company and its fortunes. Jerry found this out the hard way—pressured to put employer stock into his 401(k), Jerry lost both his salary and much of his nest egg when his small electronics firm went bust. Since even the largest corporation can be merged, acquired, or go into bankruptcy, this may be more of a risk than you should take. If you have a choice—and some companies don't give much choice—try to diversify your retirement plan investments among a variety of investment types.

The best bet is to evaluate the investment options within your employer-sponsored plan and see how they fit into your long-range financial plans as part of your total investment portfolio, both taxable and tax-deferred.

## Action Plan

**Step One:** Contribute as much as possible to an employer-sponsored retirement plan, at least up to the level of any employer match of your contributions.

**Step Two:** Choose investments to meet your long-term objectives, but do not include tax-free investments within a tax-sheltered retirement plan.

**Step Three:** Instead of concentrating retirement plan assets in stock of the company you work for, try to reduce risk by diversifying among a variety of investment vehicles.

### If You Need the Cash

If you have the opportunity to participate in a 401(k) or 403(b) plan, try to contribute as much as you can for maximum tax savings and future retirement income. I know some folks are reluctant to do so, fearing that they will be strapped for cash at some point and unable to tap the money they've put aside.

In fact, most plans offer some way to gain access to your money if you are truly in financial need, via either a loan or a hardship withdrawal. It's best to tap other sources of cash first, so that you'll have this money when you retire (it will be worth so much more after growing tax-deferred), but it can be reassuring to know that these options exist.

*Loans* are available through most large-company plans. Where available, they must follow federal rules:

• You may borrow up to half your account balance (your own contributions plus vested employer contributions), to a maximum of $50,000, or your entire balance if it is $10,000 or less. Some plans set minimum loan amounts.

- Employers must charge a "market rate" for plan loans, typically 1 or 2 percent above the current prime rate.
- If you're married, your spouse's consent may be required before you can take a loan.
- Loans must be repaid within five years, in equal installments, except that a loan used to buy your principal residence may be repaid over ten years. A one-year extension is available if you are on a leave of absence from your job, longer if your leave is for military duty. Repayment is usually accomplished through payroll deduction.
- Fail to make payments when due and the entire outstanding balance of the loan, including interest, becomes a taxable distribution. You will owe ordinary income tax plus, if you are under age 59½, a 10-percent tax penalty.
- If you retire or move on to another job, the loan must be repaid immediately—and it must be repaid from funds outside your remaining plan balance. If you are unable to do so, the loan will be considered a fully taxable distribution.

Taking a loan against a 401(k) is generally more costly than you may realize. You lose the growth on the account while paying interest—and, believe it or not, you end up paying taxes on the same money twice. You must repay the loan with after-tax dollars—and you'll pay taxes again, on the same money, when you withdraw it in retirement. Not a tax-wise move!

*Hardship withdrawals* are permitted by most plans, but the federal requirements are even more stringent than those for loans. You must have an "immediate and heavy financial need" such as uninsured medical expenses, paying a pressing college tuition bill, or preventing eviction or foreclosure. You, your spouse, and children must have no other source of cash to meet the need.

Assuming that you are allowed to make a hardship withdrawal, long-term damage to your retirement savings is inevitable. In addition, the tax consequences are severe. The withdrawal is immediately taxable, with 20 percent withheld by your employer and the balance, if any, due when you file your next income tax return. If you're under age 59½, the entire withdrawal (before taxes are deducted) is also subject to a 10-percent tax penalty—unless you are totally disabled or are using the money to pay for deductible medical expenses exceeding 7.5 percent of AGI.

A better bet, for homeowners, might be a home equity loan or line of credit. The big advantage: The interest on loans of up to $100,000 is deductible. The big risk: You're putting your home on the line, and could lose it if you are unable to repay the loan.

## THINK TWICE BEFORE TAKING A HARDSHIP WITHDRAWAL

There's not much left of a hardship withdrawal once taxes and penalties are paid. For example: A 50-year-old in a federal income tax bracket of 28 percent and a state income tax bracket of 4 percent takes a hardship withdrawal of $20,000.

| | | |
|---|---|---|
| Withdrawal: | | $20,000 |
| Minus: | | |
| Federal income tax: | $5,600 | |
| State income tax: | 800 | |
| Early withdrawal penalty: | 2,000 | |
| Total lost: | $8,400 | -$8,400 |
| Cash available from withdrawal: | | $11,600 |

## Individual Retirement Accounts

If you have earned income, you can have an Individual Retirement Account (IRA) and contribute up to $3,000 a year, $3,500 for individuals age 50 and over. These amounts are also scheduled to rise over time (see table). The contribution level is the same whether you choose a traditional IRA or its newer cousin, the Roth IRA, but there are other differences that may make one or the other a better choice for you.

## IRA CONTRIBUTIONS

| | Maximum Contribution for Individuals under Age 50 | Catch-up Contribution for Individuals Age 50 and Over |
|---|---|---|
| 2003–2004 | $3,000 | $500 |
| 2005 | $4,000 | $500 |
| 2006 | $4,000 | $1,000 |
| 2007 | $4,000 | $1,000 |
| 2008–2010 | $5,000 | $1,000 |
| 2011 and thereafter | $2,000 | 0 |

## Traditional IRAs

Traditional IRAs offer tax-deductible contributions (for eligible taxpayers) and tax-deferred growth. Earnings are taxed as ordinary income when they are withdrawn.

Contributions are fully tax deductible if you are not covered by an employer-sponsored retirement plan at work or if you are covered but your adjusted gross income is no more than $45,000 as a single taxpayer (in 2004) or $65,000 as a married taxpayer filing jointly. Contributions are partially deductible at AGI up to $55,000 for a single taxpayer and $75,000 for married taxpayers filing jointly. These amounts are scheduled to rise for the next several years.

An at-home spouse, without independent earned income, may also contribute up to $3,000 a year—even if his or her spouse is covered by an on-the-job retirement plan. These contributions are fully deductible at a family AGI of $150,000, phasing out at $160,000. Let's say you and your spouse have an adjusted gross income of $135,000 for the year, and one of you is covered by a retirement plan at work. The covered worker can't make a deductible contribution to an IRA but the spouse without an income can do so.

## BYPASSING IRA PENALTIES

Uncle Sam provides a tax break on traditional IRAs because the money is meant for retirement. Withdrawals before you reach age 59½ are therefore subject to a 10-percent tax penalty along with ordinary income tax. But there are exceptions to the penalty rules. Money may now be withdrawn early, subject to income tax but no penalty, if you:

- **die or become** disabled
- **use the money** for medical expenses in excess of 7.5 percent of your AGI
- **use the money** to pay for health insurance premiums while you are out of work
- **use up to $10,000** for the purchase of a primary residence by a first-time homebuyer (yourself or any member of your family)
- **use the money** to pay for higher education for any member of your family, or
- **take the money** in a series of substantially equal periodic payments over either your own life expectancy or the joint life expectancy of you and your beneficiary

And, in a demonstration of Uncle Sam's generous nature, there is no additional penalty if you use the money to pay a tax penalty on the IRA.

## Roth IRAs

As a relatively new sibling to the traditional IRA, the Roth IRA is a very different animal. Contributions to Roth IRAs are never deductible but earnings are never taxed, so long as the Roth IRA has been in place for at least five years and you are at least age 59½ when money is withdrawn. You may take your own contributions out at any time with no tax obligation. Better yet, if you meet income requirements (see below), you may contribute to a Roth IRA even if you are covered by an employer-sponsored retirement plan.

If you are not eligible to deduct contributions to a traditional IRA, you may want to consider a Roth IRA instead. But you may contribute the full amount to a Roth IRA only if your adjusted gross income does not exceed $95,000 if you are single or $150,000 if you are married and filing a joint return. You may not contribute to a Roth at all if your AGI exceeds $110,000 (single) or $160,000 (married, filing jointly).

If your tax bracket will be at least as high in retirement as it is now—so far as you can tell—the tax-free Roth will probably be a better bet. The Roth also has other advantages: Unlike the traditional IRA, you may continue making contributions to a Roth after you reach age 70½, so long as you still have earned income. And there is no "required beginning date" for distributions, so you don't have to start taking the money out at any specific time. In fact, if you have enough other retirement income, you may leave a Roth in place for your family. (Chapters 5 and 6 have more details on retirement plan distributions, when you leave a job and when you retire.)

## Timing Is All

If you have not yet made an IRA contribution for last year, consider doubling up now. Make your contribution for last year before April 15 (you have until April 15 even if you have received an extension to file your income tax return later in the year) and, at the same time, make a contribution for the current year. This way you'll reap a double deduction for this year. Then make your future contributions as early each year as possible to benefit from tax-deferred growth throughout the remainder of the year.

Deductions for IRA contributions may be taken even if you file a short form and even if you don't itemize deductions. Unlike most other deductions, IRA contributions are "above-the-line" deductions that reduce your adjusted gross income.

## Action Plan

**Step One:** Decide whether a traditional IRA or a Roth IRA better meets your needs.

**Step Two:** Make your IRA contribution for last year right away, if you haven't already done so.

**Step Three:** At the same time, make your IRA contribution for this year.

**Step Four:** Going forward, make your contributions as early each year as possible.

### Making a Switch

If you have many years ahead before you retire, it may be worth converting a traditional IRA to a Roth IRA so that all future growth is tax-free. You can make this conversion if your adjusted gross income (in the year of the conversion) does not exceed $100,000 (married or single). If your income is normally a bit higher, consider postponing a year-end bonus or adjusting your investment strategy to temporarily minimize current income.

To make a conversion, simply notify the institution holding your IRA that you want the account retitled as a Roth IRA; then follow up to make sure the appropriate paperwork has been completed.

When you convert an existing IRA to a Roth IRA, however, you are actually withdrawing the money from the traditional IRA. There is no tax penalty on a conversion, but withdrawals are subject to tax and you will have an immediate income-tax bill. To avoid a large tax bill in a single year, if your IRA holds a substantial sum, convert a portion of your IRA each year to spread the tax burden over several years. Either way, try to pay the tax from other sources and not from the IRA itself.

And be careful: The amount converted increases your adjusted gross income, raising your taxes for the year of the conversion. The amount of AGI, in turn, has a direct impact on the taxes you owe. For example, as discussed earlier, if AGI exceeds $139,500 for the 2003 tax year (married or single), you start to lose the benefit of some itemized deductions.

## Undoing a Roth Conversion

Change your mind? Undoing a conversion, in IRS-speak, is called a "recharacterization." The most frequent reason for recharacterization, in the early days of the Roth, was finding that income for the year actually exceeded the $100,000 threshold. At this writing, another reason is the decline in value of the converted IRA due to stock market losses.

As Richard J. Berry Jr., Michael B. Kennedy, and Bernard S. Kent write in *PricewaterhouseCoopers Guide to the New Tax Rules,* investment losses can make it a good time for conversion because "the tax cost will be based on the low valuations at the time of the conversion." At the same time, if you converted to a Roth and *then* the account's value dropped significantly, you might recharacterize so as not to pay the tax on the phantom value. William was pleased with his decision to switch to a

Roth—until his $100,000 account lost $30,000 of its value in the stock market downturn of 2002. When he realized that he still owed tax on the full $100,000—the value at the time of conversion—he quickly recharacterized to a traditional IRA to eliminate the tax bill.

Conversions may be recharacterized until October 15 of the following year, either via an extension of the original filing date or—if you already filed your return for the year—with an amended return. If circumstances should change and make it desirable to have a Roth, the account can be "reconverted." But you can't seesaw back and forth. To reconvert, you must wait until the later of

1. the beginning of the tax year following the year in which the account was converted to a Roth IRA, or
2. 30 days after the date on which the Roth IRA was recharacterized as a traditional IRA.

---

### AN EXTRA DEDUCTION

Annual maintenance fees for IRAs and other retirement plans are deductible—but only if paid separately and not out of the retirement account. Include separately paid fees as a miscellaneous itemized deduction on Schedule A of Form 1040.

---

## Retirement Plans for the Self-employed

If you are self-employed, you won't have the luxury of employer-paid retirement benefits—or the tax breaks that go along with making your own sizable contributions to an employer-sponsored plan. You may open an IRA, of course, but contributions limited to $3,000 a year won't produce much retirement income. Fortunately, you have other ways to build future income while deriving current tax benefits—you may establish a SEP-IRA, a Keogh plan, or a SIMPLE plan.

## SEP-IRAs

This variation on the plain-vanilla traditional IRA has one distinct advantage: Instead of just $3,000 a year, you may contribute up to 25 percent of compensation to a maximum of $40,000. The acronym stands for Simplified Employee Plans—and, indeed, these plans are easy to establish at most financial institutions and easy to administer. You can vary your contributions from year to year. There is no requirement to file an annual tax return for the plan. And, like other IRAs, SEPs can be established and funded until the date of filing your tax return.

A possible drawback to SEP plans may be that, once you have employees, you must make contributions on behalf of any employee who is at least age 21 and has worked for you, even part-time, in three of the preceding five years. Those contributions immediately belong to the employees, who invest them as they choose.

## Keogh Plans

These qualified retirement plans for the self-employed resemble corporate retirement plans in many important ways—including the fact that employees must be included once they have reached age 21 and have worked for you for one year. Once employees are included (unlike the less regulated SEP-IRAs), these plans are subject to all the protections—and the paperwork—of federal law. Annual tax returns are required if the plan includes employees and, even if you are the only participant, once assets exceed $100,000.

Keogh plans come in two flavors: defined contribution and

defined benefit. Both must be opened before the end of the calendar year, although contributions may be made until the tax filing date the following year.

- *Defined contribution plans* are like corporate profit-sharing plans. You may contribute up to 100 percent of pretax income up to a maximum of $40,000. You may contribute less in years when money is tight. (Until the 2001 Tax Act, you needed both a profit-sharing plan and a money-purchase plan in order to contribute the maximum amount. Money-purchase plans are no longer needed.) Defined contribution plans can be easily established at most banks, brokerage firms, and mutual funds.
- *Defined benefit plans* are like corporate pension plans. They must be funded to reach a desired benefit level at a designated retirement age, a target that can permit much larger annual contributions. For older self-employed individuals with enough dollars to spare, defined benefit plans offer the largest contributions, the most tax savings, and the greatest buildup of future retirement income. However, they are complicated and expensive to set up and administer. Actuarial and accounting help is needed.

## MOONLIGHTING

Even if you run your own business while holding down a salaried job, and even if you are covered by a retirement plan at your full-time job, you may open a retirement plan for self-employment income. Whether you choose a SEP-IRA, a Keogh plan, or a SIMPLE plan, you can reduce your taxable income by the amount of your contributions. At the same time, you'll be building a tax-deferred nest egg for retirement.

## SIMPLE Plans

In a third possibility for amassing retirement savings, the SIMPLE (Savings Incentive Match Plans for Employees) plan resembles a streamlined 401(k) plan designed especially for businesses with fewer than one hundred employees. SIMPLE plans are not as desirable for many sole proprietors because the maximum per-employee contribution is $9,000 in 2004, with a catch-up contribution of $1,500 for employees age 50 and over. (SEP-IRAs and Keogh plans do not permit catch-up contributions but have larger base contributions). However, you may contribute this much for yourself even if it is your entire income from self-employment.

If you have employees, you must make dollar-for-dollar matching contributions on their behalf. You have two choices: You may contribute

1. up to a maximum of 3 percent of pay for each employee who chooses to participate in the plan, or
2. a flat 2 percent of pay for each employee, whether or not the employee chooses to participate.

You may also make a 3-percent matching contribution for yourself, bringing your potential contribution for yourself up to $15,000—but only if your compensation is at least $200,000 (3 percent of $200,000 is $6,000).

A SIMPLE plan is easy to start and to administer, you can skip an annual contribution if money is tight, and it may be the best bet if your self-employment income is minimal or erratic.

## Action Plan

**Step One:** Decide how much you can contribute toward your own future retirement from self-employment income.

**Step Two:** Decide how much you can contribute on behalf of employees.

**Step Three:** Open a SEP-IRA, Keogh plan, or SIMPLE plan.

**Step Four:** Decide how to invest your contributions within the plan.

## Another Choice: Annuities

Whether you are employed or self-employed, once you've made maximum contributions to tax-qualified retirement plans, you may want to consider purchasing an annuity to set aside more tax-deferred income for retirement.

Annuities resemble tax-qualified plans but have significant differences as well. The similarities include the fact that earnings grow tax-deferred until the money is withdrawn, when it is taxed at ordinary income rates. In addition, because the tax deferral is meant to encourage retirement savings, there is generally a tax penalty if money is withdrawn before you reach age 59½. On the other hand, there is no ceiling on how much you may contribute to an annuity. Contributions are never tax deductible. And there is no "required beginning date" for distributions; money may be left in an annuity well beyond the age 70½ beginning date for IRA withdrawals.

Annuities are flexible instruments; they may be immediate or deferred, fixed or variable. Immediate annuities, with distributions starting within a year of purchase, are often purchased with a lump sum from an employer retirement plan or money from the sale of a business. Deferred annuities, with a long accumulation period before distributions begin, may be purchased with a lump sum or with periodic contributions over time.

Fixed annuities grow at a fixed rate set by the issuer, a rate often guaranteed for three to five years and then subject to change. The return on variable annuities is pegged to the performance of underlying "subaccounts" of your choice. Subaccounts resemble mutual funds and are often offered by investment companies offering comparable mutual funds to the general public.

Variable annuities often have sizable up-front fees. Both variable and fixed annuities typically have substantial withdrawal penalties within the first few years. Annuities also have tax consequences. If you die during the accumulation period of a deferred annuity, the money will be part of your potentially taxable estate. Any excess beyond your contributions—the money earned on your contributions—will also be subject to income tax. There are also tax consequences when you withdraw money from an annuity. See Chapter 6 for details.

---

### TAX TIPS FOR APRIL

- **Pay your taxes**—or arrange for an automatic extension—by April 15.
- **Pay your first-quarter** estimate, if due, by April 15.
- **Defer tax on investment income** through tax-sheltered retirement plans.
- **Select the investments** within your retirement plan to meet your long-term goals and tolerance for risk.
- **Consider an annuity** to supplement retirement income from qualified plans.

## CHAPTER 5

# May
# Your Job and Your Taxes

If you hold a salaried job, with income tax withheld from each paycheck, you may think that's all you need to know. In fact, whether you are employed or self-employed, there are a host of tax issues you need to be aware of—and tax-saving strategies you can put to good use.

For employees, there are issues involving fringe benefits, job-related expenses, stock options, and job change. For the self-employed, especially those working in offices at home, there are major questions about what is deductible and what is not.

## Fringe Benefits

On-the-job benefits at the largest corporations range from on-site child-care facilities to elder-care referral services. Probably the two most important benefits, however, are health insurance and retirement benefits.

*Health insurance* premiums paid by an employer are not taxable income for employees. Health insurance benefits are also not taxable. If you're fortunate enough to be eligible for a flexible spending account (see page 83), you can reap still more tax benefits by putting pretax dollars aside for uninsured medical expenses.

*Disability income,* the insurance that replaces income lost because of a serious accident or long-term illness, is a different story. Employer-paid premiums are not taxable income but benefits under employer-paid policies are subject to tax. Think about this when you decide to skip buying an individual disability income policy. In addition, because employer-paid benefits are typically capped at 60 percent of earnings, paying tax on those benefits leaves you with less than half your accustomed income. If you buy an individual disability income policy and pay for it with after-tax dollars, any benefits you collect will be free from income tax. Even if you are included in a good disability plan at work, therefore, you may want to consider buying an individual policy to provide supplemental income. An individual policy also lets you buy more years of coverage.

Other on-the-job benefits that are typically nontaxable income for recipients include

- employer-paid *education assistance* of up to $5,250 a year, whether undergraduate or graduate-level and whether or not the education is job-related
- group term *life insurance* up to $50,000; additional amounts are taxed as income
- a *company car* used exclusively for business; any personal use of the same car is treated as taxable income
- employer-paid *adoption assistance*
- the use of a *fitness center* that is at the employer's location and is not open to the general public

In addition, pretax income may be set aside for *commuting costs.* If you use a van pool or public transportation to get to work, you may set aside up to $100 a month to cover the cost. If you drive to work, up to $190 a month may be set aside to cover the cost of parking. Use both your own car and mass transit, perhaps by driving to a park-and-ride lot, and the set-aside may be as much as $290 per month. That's $3,480 of annual income that will remain untaxed. In the 28-percent tax bracket, that's an annual saving of $974.

In general, the cost of your daily travel from home to work is not a deductible expense. But travel between business locations *is* deductible. If you leave the office to go to a meeting at a client's office or to go to the airport for an out-of-town trip, the cost is deductible at 36 cents a mile (in 2003) plus parking and tolls. (Taxpayers with home offices have more flexibility in deducting travel costs; see page 97.)

## Flex-plans

Flexible spending accounts, part of the benefits package at many large corporations, offer significant tax savings. These plans let covered employees set aside pretax earnings to pay for qualified medical expenses and/or dependent care. With a medical plan, you set aside money to pay for uninsured out-of-pocket expenses; dependent care can pick up a portion of preschool or day-care costs. Although enrollment periods are typically in the fall, you can change your contribution schedule earlier in the year if there are changes in your personal situation.

The money you contribute is not subject to federal income tax, FICA (Social Security) tax, or most state and local income taxes. Money you collect from the plans is not taxable. The result: If you are in the 28-percent federal tax bracket, $2,000 put in a flex-plan will buy the same goods and services as more than $3,000 of regular income.

**Dependent care plans** have a federal contribution ceiling of $5,000 a year. Dependent care accounts can be used to pay for the care of children under age 13 by a baby-sitter, in a day-care center, or in a before-school or after-school program. The accounts can also pay toward the care of older children, spouses, or parents who are disabled.

One caveat: You cannot use a dependent care flex-plan and

also claim the federal child-care tax credit of $1,000. Do your calculations carefully to see which way you'll come out ahead, remembering that the child-care tax credit phases out at a modified AGI over $110,000 for married individuals filing jointly and $75,000 for single taxpayers and heads of households. Also: If you and your spouse both have dependent care accounts, your combined expenditure ceiling—the amount that is allowed on your federal income-tax return—is still limited to $5,000.

**Medical expense plans** have no federal ceiling on contributions, but most plans limit annual contributions to $5,000.

Medical flex-plans can be used to cover deductibles and co-payments under health insurance. They can also pay for medical expenses that are not covered by health insurance, so long as those expenditures would be deductible on the federal income-tax return. Examples include eye exams, eyeglasses and contact lenses, hearing exams and hearing aids, and dental costs. Since medical costs are deductible only to the extent that they exceed 7.5 percent of AGI—a hurdle impossible for most people to clear—a flex-plan puts most people way ahead. (Chapter 11 has more details on medical deductions.)

Health spending accounts have another major advantage because medical expenses can be reimbursed even before the account is fully funded. Let's say you sign up to put in $300 a month, then need surgery in March that costs $3,000. You've put in only $900—but as long as your contributions for the year will cover the cost, you are entitled to full reimbursement right away. This feature amounts to an interest-free loan from the plan.

With either type of flex-plan, you decide how much to contribute each year, up to the maximum. Dependent care is easy to figure; if you pay for child care, you know how much it will be. Medical care is more of a moving target. But let's say you know that your 10-year-old will need braces next year, to the tune of $2,000. You also expect to need about $400 for other uninsured medical expenses. Based on these calculations, you put $200 a month into your flex-plan. If you are in the 28-percent federal tax bracket, paying 7.65 percent in combined Social Security and Medicare tax and an assumed 3 percent in state income tax, you'll save almost $800.

Choose your contribution amounts with care. You may make a change only once a year, typically in the fall, *unless* the company changes its benefit plan or there is a change—such as marriage, divorce, or a new baby—in your personal circumstances. For the most part, flex-plans are a "use it or lose it" proposition. If you overestimate how much you'll need, and don't spend the money in the plan by year-end, you forfeit whatever is left.

## Action Plan

**Step One:** Obtain an enrollment form and sign up for a flex-plan offered by your employer as soon as you are eligible.

**Step Two:** Estimate how much you will use in the following year for child care or medical expenses such as day care or a baby-sitter, eyeglasses, or uninsured dental care.

**Step Three:** Contribute the amount you expect to use.

**Step Four:** Use up the money in your plan before year-end.

## Unreimbursed Employee Expenses

As an employee, you may sometimes incur expenses directly related to your job but not reimbursed by your employer. Some of these expenses may be deductible, benefiting the bottom line on your tax return. But the IRS takes a hard line—especially when it comes to computers and cell phones—requiring proof that the expense is necessary to do your job. Even when an insurance agent needed a laptop to develop sales presentations because office computers were rarely available, the IRS held that buying the computer was optional and therefore not deductible.

*Education* comes under special rules. If you pay for your own further education and are not reimbursed by your employer, the expenses are deductible if the education

- is required by your employer or the law to keep your present salary, status, or job, or
- maintains or improves skills needed in your present work

If the education qualifies under the above rules, you may deduct associated travel and transportation expenses along with half the cost of necessary meals.

Education is *not* deductible if it is needed to meet the minimum educational requirements of your present trade or business, or if it is designed to prepare you for a new occupation. Here, too, there are gray areas. The IRS has allowed deductions for teachers moving from one subject specialty to another. It allowed a practicing dentist to deduct the costs associated with learning to be an orthodontist, holding that he had improved his skills as a dentist rather than learning a new profession. Yet the IRS specifically disqualifies review courses designed to prepare for the bar exam or CPA licensing.

If you use your *automobile* for business and your employer does not reimburse expenses, you may be entitled to some tax write-offs as well based on either the actual cost of operating your car for business or a per-mile amount (36 cents for the 2003 tax year). The per-mile count is easier and works out well for most taxpayers. It's possible to switch from per-mile to actual cost, but you are not allowed to take actual cost and then shift to per-mile deductions on the same car in subsequent years.

If the car is used exclusively for business, the tax calculations are easy. If you also use it to run personal errands or go for a Sunday drive, you must keep track of the business mileage. The easiest way is to keep a notebook in the car, recording the odometer readings at the beginning and end of every business trip together with the purpose of the trip. If you are an employee, you claim the deduction on Form 2106 with a break-down of business and personal use. Note, however, that automobile expenses are deductible only to the extent that—together with other miscellaneous itemized deductions—they exceed 2 percent of your adjusted gross income.

---

### TWO JOBS? TOO MUCH SOCIAL SECURITY WITHHELD?

Every employer is required to withhold FICA taxes for Social Security and Medicare from employees' wages, up to each year's wage cap ($87,000 for 2003). If you hold two jobs during the year, earning more than the wage cap, you could wind up with too much withheld. If this happens to you, you may claim a credit for the excess amount against any federal income tax that is due when you file your tax return for the year. If you are not required to file an income-tax return, you may file a special refund claim to have the excess returned.

---

## Employee Stock Options

Stock options surged in importance throughout the 1990s, as dot-com companies and other start-ups rewarded employees with an ownership slice in the company. Once reserved for executives at the top of the corporate ladder, options became part of compensation for large numbers of midlevel workers.

Many employees became very wealthy by exercising stock options at vastly appreciated prices. Then the stock market stumbled. With the downturn, stock options largely faded from the radar screen. But they are still offered by some companies, and many employees still hold them from the glory days, so—with myriad tax ramifications—they are still well worth discussing.

Options offer employees the right to purchase shares of the employer's common stock at a stated price during a specified period of time. The exercise price (the price at which shares of stock may be purchased) is typically the market value of the stock at the time the options are granted. Employees holding options hope for appreciation in the stock price so that they can purchase shares of higher value at the built-in exercise price.

If options are not exercised by the designated date, typically ten years after the grant, they expire and become worthless. They also become worthless—and are called "underwater"—if the market value of the stock drops below the exercise price. In fact, if you exercise the option and the price of the stock then drops below the purchase price before you can lock in profits by selling, you can end up owing taxes on the options while realizing a loss on the investment. This is not a happy outcome, although losses on stock options can be used to offset other investment gains and any excess can offset up to $3,000 of other income.

Options come in two flavors, with different tax implications.

**Nonqualified stock options** (NQSOs) are more common because the employer—the issuer of the options—receives a tax deduction for any appreciation in the share price between the time the options are granted and the time they are exercised (used to buy shares of stock). Employees pay tax at capital-gains rates only if the stock price goes up after the options are exercised and the stock is then held for at least a year. Meanwhile, when nonqualified options are exercised, the employee owes tax at ordinary income rates on the difference between the value of the stock and the option price. Employers must withhold federal income and FICA taxes to satisfy this obligation.

**Incentive stock options** (ISOs) are not treated as income when exercised but do offer employees the advantage of having profits—the difference between the exercise price and the subsequent sale price—taxed at the lower capital-gains rate. However, because ISOs are taxed at the lower capital-gains rate, they are also subject to more restrictions. For example, you get the tax advantage only if you do not sell the stock for at least one year from the exercise date and at least two years from the date of the initial option grant. Sell earlier and any tax will be at higher ordinary income rates. In addition, should there be sizable profits, the income may make you subject to the alternative minimum tax (see Chapter 12) and result in a higher tax bill.

### LOST YOUR JOB?

Income may be down, yet your tax bill may be up. Jobless workers have been unpleasantly surprised to find that severance pay and unemployment benefits are taxed as part of total income. Keep track of job-hunting expenses, however, since costs such as résumé printing, postage, and travel are deductible and may reduce your tax burden.

## Job Change

There are at least two tax issues involved when you change jobs. The first—especially important if you've lost your job in the downsizing of the last few years—is the deductibility of job-hunting costs and job-related moving expenses. The second is what to do with accumulated retirement savings when you leave a job, whether or not you immediately find another position.

### Job-hunting Expenses

Some expenses incurred in a job search are deductible so long as you are looking for a new job in your present occupation—whether or not you actually find a job. You may face a challenge by the IRS, however, if you take an extended vacation between leaving one job and looking for a new one. And you may lose the deduction if the IRS decides that you were making a career change—although the IRS doesn't always win this battle. When a CPA holding a salaried job decided to go out on his own and deducted expenses associated with deciding if he could make a successful career change, the IRS turned him down. The U.S. Tax Court disagreed, holding that job-search expenses were a justifiable deduction whether the CPA was seeking work as an employee or setting up a new practice.

These are the job-search expenses that are deductible, to the extent that—along with other miscellaneous deductions—they exceed 2 percent of adjusted gross income:

- employment agency fees
- outplacement and career counseling
- résumé preparation, including the costs of typing, printing, and mailing
- travel and transportation expenses incurred in seeking a new job, including meals, lodging, and local transportation where a trip is focused on job search
- fees for legal and tax advice relating to employment contracts
- long-distance telephone calls to prospective employers
- the cost of placing an ad or buying publications to review job listings

## Moving Costs

Moving is generally a nondeductible personal expense. Move because you're changing jobs, however, and much of the cost may be deductible. Because moving expenses are deducted from gross income, you can benefit from the deduction while using the standard deduction. You do not have to itemize.

But you must meet all three of the following conditions:

- The move must be closely related in time to the start of work. The IRS generally allows a year, although special circumstances—if, for example, your family remains in the former location until a child graduates from high school—may extend the period.
- Your new place of work must be at least fifty miles farther from your former home than your last place of work was from your former home.
- Employed or self-employed, you must work full-time in the new location (not necessarily at the same job) for at least thirty-nine weeks during the year following the move. If you are self-employed, you must also work full-time for at least seventy-eight weeks out of the first twenty-four months.

If you qualify, you may deduct the cost of moving yourself and your family (travel and lodging but no longer—alas—meals) and the cost of moving your household goods and personal possessions. The check you write to the moving company is deductible and so is the cost of disconnecting utilities in order to move household appliances. If you use your own car to make the move, you may deduct either actual expenses or a flat 12 cents per mile (for 2003). You may take the deduction for the year you move, even if you have not yet met the thirty-nine-week or seventy-eight-week test.

### Retirement Savings

One of the big issues, when you change jobs in midcareer, is what to do with accumulated retirement savings. If you have been making pretax contributions to a 401(k) or other defined contribution plan, the money (with the accumulated interest and/or dividends it has earned) belongs to you. If your employer has been making matching contributions, that money will belong to you if you have been employed long enough to meet vesting requirements.

If you have less than $5,000 accumulated in an employer-sponsored retirement plan when you leave the job, you will probably have to take the distribution in cash. If you have more than $5,000, you may be offered several choices about what to do with the money:

1. Take it in a lump sum.
2. Take it in substantially equal periodic payments over your life expectancy.
3. Leave the money in place, if the plan permits, so that it remains invested and continues to grow.
4. Transfer the money to a plan sponsored by your new employer, if that plan will accept the transfer.
5. Transfer the money to a rollover IRA.

Some of these choices are better than others, particularly in light of the tax consequences. Here are some things to consider before you decide what to do.

*Taking a lump sum* is typically the worst possible choice because you must pay income tax immediately on the full amount, with your employer withholding 20 percent. Worse, you will lose all future growth in your retirement nest egg.

This double whammy means that you should really think twice before taking a lump sum. If you take $10,000 out of a 401(k) plan and pay federal income tax on it at 28 percent, you lose $2,800 right off the top. If you're under age 59½ and owe a 10-percent tax penalty, that's another $1,000 gone (but not forgotten). Instead, if you keep the $10,000 growing tax-deferred, either by leaving it in the 401(k) plan or rolling it into an IRA, you'll have $21,500 after ten years if the money is invested at a steady return of 8 percent. That's if you never add another penny. Keep working and contributing and your retirement nest egg will continue to grow.

---

### BYPASSING PENALTIES

The 10-percent tax penalty, normally imposed on withdrawals before age 59½, can be avoided if you qualify under a set of specific IRS exceptions. These include

1. becoming totally disabled
2. using the money for medical expenses exceeding 7.5 percent of your adjusted gross income
3. taking the money in substantially equal periodic payments over your lifetime

In addition, if you are at least age 55 when you leave your job, there won't be a penalty. And, if you must distribute the money under a qualified domestic relations order as part of a divorce settlement, the tax is paid by the recipient and not by you.

---

**Taking substantially equal periodic distributions over your lifetime** may be one of the least understood of the distribution options. Here's how it works. At any age, and whether or not you retire, you can eliminate the 10-percent early withdrawal penalty by electing to take your distribution in the form of substantially equal periodic distributions based on your life expectancy or the joint life expectancy of you and your beneficiary. But you're not really locked in for life. You must continue the payments for at least five years or until you reach age 59½, whichever is later. While you can skip the 10-percent tax penalty, you will still owe tax at ordinary income rates on each distribution.

**Tax tip:** If you have already arranged substantially equal periodic payments in fixed amounts and have seen your account balance shrink in the recent market downturn, the IRS will let you change to distributions based on the value of the account each year.

**Leaving the money in place,** if your employer's plan permits you to do so, may be a good choice if you are happy with the investment options under the plan. Be aware, though, that employers really don't like the administrative headaches involved in keeping former employees in the retirement plan. As a result, many company plans require you to withdraw the money within five years after leaving the job, investment choices may be curtailed, and beneficiary designations may be limited.

**Transferring the money to a new employer's plan** may be a good choice—if the new plan permits immediate participation. Many have a waiting period and, if this is the case, you may want to use a rollover IRA as a temporary parking place for the money.

**Transferring the money to a rollover IRA** is the best choice for most people, under most circumstances, because it keeps your options open. The money will continue to grow tax-deferred. In contrast to the six to ten investment choices available in most 401(k) plans, you will be able to invest in a wide range of individual stocks and bonds, mutual funds, and certificates of deposit. And, if you keep the rollover IRA separate from any other IRAs you may have, you will be able to transfer the money to an employer plan at a later date.

To move the money into an IRA without owing any immediate income tax, have your employer transfer it directly to the IRA custodian. If the money passes through your hands, even temporarily, your employer will be required to withhold 20 percent in taxes. You can get the money back, but not until after you file your federal income tax return the following year. Meanwhile, you have to come up with the money to deposit 100 percent of the rollover into the IRA or you will be hit with both income tax and, if you're under age 59½, a possible 10-percent tax penalty.

**Tax tip:** Retirement presents some of the same options for dealing with retirement savings, but there are some differences. See Chapter 6.

---

### COMPANY STOCK AND
### AN IRA ROLLOVER

If appreciated company stock makes up a large part of your 401(k) plan, you may want to roll it into a taxable account instead of into a tax-deferred IRA. You'll have to pay immediate tax at ordinary income rates on the value of the shares at the time they were purchased by the 401(k) plan—but you'll be able to pay the lower capital-gains rate on appreciation from the plan's purchase date until the date you sell. In addition, because there are no required distribution rules on taxable accounts, you can hold on to the stock and leave it to your family. If instead you leave the company stock in a tax-deferred account and it continues to appreciate, you will have to start withdrawals on the April 1 after the year in which you reach age 70½. And you can expect to pay much more in tax—the difference, at this writing, between a capital-gains tax of no more than 15 percent and ordinary income tax that can run as high as 35 percent. (For more on "net unrealized appreciation," see pages 106–107.)

---

## Taxes and the Self-employed

Work for yourself and you're in a special position. You must pay your own income taxes by filing quarterly estimates. If you earn more than $400 a year, you must pay the entire FICA tax, the 15.3 percent of net income (12.4 percent for Social Security and 2.9 percent for Medicare) that is divided between employer and employee for wage earners. However, 50 percent of the tax is then deductible from gross income.

You must also do without the benefits taken for granted by employees. As a sole proprietor, you have no paid vacation, employer-paid retirement plan, or on-the-job health insurance. However, you may deduct contributions to self-funded retirement plans (see Chapter 4). You may also deduct the expenses associated with running your business.

## Business Expenses

Whether or not you maintain an office at home, when you are self-employed you are entitled to deductions for your costs of doing business. These expenses include

- direct costs such as postage and supplies associated with your business
- up to $100,000 per year in capital expenditures for such items as computer equipment and vehicles used in your business. This larger limit, a product of the 2003 tax act, applies to tax years from 2003 through 2005 (with the $100,000 amount adjusted for inflation in 2004 and 2005).
- the entire cost of your health insurance premiums, so long as you are not eligible for an employer-subsidized plan (through your own employment or that of your spouse) and the premiums do not exceed net business earnings for the year. Tax tip: Hire your spouse or children to work in your business and premiums for their health insurance will be deductible too.
- the cost of meals and entertainment generated in the course of doing business—but only up to 50 percent of the actual expenditure. Keep good records, including receipts indicating whom you took out to lunch and what business matters were discussed.

- actual expenses or a per-mile deduction for the use of your automobile or other vehicle in your business. If you have a home office, you are ahead of salaried workers in this respect. While most taxpayers can't deduct commuting costs, the U.S. Tax Court has ruled that you can deduct the cost of travel from your home office to other business locations. Drive to your customers' places of business from your home office and the cost is deductible.

---

### HOME OFFICE AS RED FLAG

Some taxpayers refuse to claim the home office deduction because they believe it produces an almost automatic audit of the tax return. This is not so. If you are legitimately entitled to a home office deduction, you should take it. But you should also be scrupulous about keeping records, maintaining calendars, ledgers, and receipts to document all the deductions you claim. IRS Publication 587 has more information.

---

### Home Office Expenses

Deductible business expenses include expenses associated with an office at home—so long as you meet these conditions:

1. the office must be used exclusively and regularly for your business or as a place to meet customers as part of your business
2. you have no other location in which to manage your business
3. no personal activity takes place in the space set aside for business—the space does not contain a pullout couch for overnight guests or a TV your family watches in the evening

The definition of a deductible home office has been loosened considerably from the days—not all that long ago—when an office had to be the "principal" place of business. Under that interpretation, plumbers or interior designers or computer consultants who spent most of their working hours in other people's homes and offices could not deduct expenses associated with the home office where they maintained records, returned client phone calls, and did their billing. Today you can perform in a symphony orchestra but practice at home and claim a home office. You can spend most of your waking hours working in a hospital setting but do your billing at home and claim a home office. You can even spend four days a week in another office but meet customers or clients one day a week at home and claim a home office.

With a home office meeting IRS regulations, you can deduct two types of expenses, direct and indirect. You may claim direct expenditures in full. An example would be built-in bookcases or having the office painted. You may also deduct a proportionate share of indirect expenses such as utilities, homeowners insurance, and maintenance related to the office. You may not deduct the basic cost of the first phone line into your home, although you may claim toll calls made in connection with your business; the cost of a second line is deductible. To claim home office expenses, attach Form 8829 to the Schedule C you file for self-employment income.

## Action Plan

**Step One:** To determine the amount you may deduct for a home office, figure out the square footage of your home and then the square footage occupied by your office within the home. For example, if your rooms are approximately the same size and you use one room of an eight-room house to manage your business and for nothing else—never accommodating

## Action Plan

overnight guests on the pullout couch—you may take 12.5 percent of these household expenses as a home office deduction. If you live in a small apartment and can't use one room exclusively for business, you may divide a room as long as you clearly mark the area designated as an office. Use a partition or put masking tape on the floor, but don't use the office area for anything else.

**Step Two:** List your deductions in this order:

1. Expenses that are deductible because you own a home, whether or not you take a home office deduction. If you use 20 percent of your home as an office, then 20 percent of your real estate taxes and mortgage interest may be claimed as a deduction on your Schedule C; the balance appears on Schedule A. While you can deduct these expenses without a home office, taking the deductions on Schedule C is preferable. Doing so reduces your net self-employment income and therefore the amount you pay toward Social Security and Medicare.

2. Direct business expenses such as office supplies, secretarial help, postage, and telephone that you could claim whether or not you claim a deduction for a home office.

3. Household expenses benefiting your home office, such as cleaning services and insurance and roof repair, in proportion to the amount of space used. In reasoning known only to the IRS, you may deduct a portion of snow removal but not landscaping or lawn services.

4. Depreciation of the portion of the home used for the business. This depreciation will be "recaptured" when you sell the house, with tax then due at the rate of 25 percent. (For more on home sales, see Chapter 7.)

## MAKING MONEY AT HOME

Mortgage interest and real estate taxes are always deductible. Direct business expenses are deductible too, whether or not your business earns a profit. Indirect expenses—the outlay related to having your office as part of your home—are deductible only if your business makes money. If you can't claim all of your deductions because you haven't made enough money in a given year, you may carry unused deductions into succeeding tax years. Sooner or later, however, unless you have income exceeding expenses in three out of five years, you will lose the deductions.

## TAX TIPS FOR MAY

- **Many job-related fringe benefits** are tax-free.
- **Flexible spending accounts** let you put aside pretax pay toward medical expenses and child care.
- **Unreimbursed employee expenses** may be deductible.
- **Nonqualified stock options** and incentive stock options have different tax consequences.
- **Job-hunting and job-related** expenses may be deductible.
- **Retirement savings can** continue to accumulate tax-deferred when you change jobs.
- **Self-employed taxpayers** may deduct direct business expenses and the expenses associated with a home office.

# CHAPTER 6

# June: Moving On
## Retirement and Beyond

When you're ready to retire—or just beginning to think about it—taxes take on a whole new meaning. The strategic planning you do right now will affect how much tax you pay on your retirement income—and how much tax your family eventually pays on your estate. Procrastinating can mean you will pay a whole lot more.

It would be nice if taxes would disappear when we stop working, but they don't and they won't. In fact, you may have to start filing quarterly estimated tax returns for the first time in your life. Tax may have been conveniently withheld from your paycheck all your working life but the responsibility to pay taxes—and pay them on time—falls on your shoulders once that paycheck stops.

Contrary to what you may think, in fact, your taxes may not fall in retirement. Your investment income, pension, and Social Security—along with any postretirement wages, should you work full- or part-time—may put you in as high a tax bracket as you were before retirement. If you know that you will be in a higher bracket—not easy to predict, since tax law and brackets change constantly—you may want to tap retirement funds earlier rather than waiting until you must take distributions. More on this later.

# Estimated Tax

Estimated tax payments must be made on a quarterly basis if you expect to owe at least $1,000 in tax for the year. There is a "safe harbor"—and you can skip the quarterly payments—if a combination of withheld tax and tax credits adds up to at least 90 percent of the tax you will owe for this year or 100 percent of the tax paid for the prior year. If your adjusted gross income is more than $150,000 as a married couple filing jointly, you must pay at least 110 percent of last year's tax to avoid underpayment penalties.

Be especially careful in the year you retire. Your tax bill may be higher than in years before or after if you receive a lump sum severance payment or accept a lump sum distribution from a retirement plan and do not immediately roll it into an IRA. If you retire midyear, you must also consider any amount withheld from salary before you retire. When it comes to determining whether underpayment penalties apply, Sidney Kess and Barbara E. Weltman write in the *CCH Retirement Planning Guide*, "Withholding is treated as having been made 25 percent in each estimated tax period even if actually withheld early or late in the year."

There is a possible reprieve from underpayment penalties in the year you retire—if you are over age 62, you may apply for a waiver of the penalty if there was "reasonable cause" for the underpayment. (A waiver may also be requested if you become disabled or are affected by a natural disaster.) But a waiver must be requested; you can't simply neglect a payment you know is due and expect to avoid penalties. To request the waiver, file Form 2210 with a statement of the reason for the underpayment.

**Tax tip:** You may be able to skip estimated payments by electing voluntary withholding on Social Security retirement benefits and retirement plan distributions. For Social Security benefits, file Form W-4V with the Social Security Administration. For retirement distributions, file Form W-4P with the administrator or custodian of your pension plan. You can even elect to have additional tax withheld if doing so will eliminate the need to file quarterly estimated taxes on other income such as interest and dividends. And you can stop withholding, if you change your mind at a later date, by filing a new form.

As you move into retirement, short-term planning focuses on retirement distributions. Looking ahead, estate planning can minimize taxes for your heirs.

## Retirement Income Choices

Among the decisions that should be on your immediate agenda:

- how to take benefits from company plans
- how to take distributions from Individual Retirement Accounts
- when to start Social Security retirement benefits
- how to take distributions from an annuity

The decisions you make in each area will have a significant impact on your retirement income—and on the taxes due on that income.

### Company Plans

Employer-sponsored retirement plans come in two flavors: *defined benefit* and *defined contribution*. When it's time to take the money from either type of plan, it's also time to weigh the tax consequences of the various distribution choices.

Traditional defined benefit pension plans pay guaranteed retirement benefits based on age, earnings, and length of service. If you are covered by a defined benefit plan—increasingly rare these days—your employer must give you a document called a Summary Plan Description (SPD). This document spells out how benefits are calculated, when they are vested, and when they will begin.

Most defined benefit plans pay benefits in the form of monthly checks for life. Some offer retirees the option of a lump-sum payment at retirement.

Monthly checks offer a distinct advantage: You will never outlive the income. In fact, if you elect monthly payments and are married, you must take the money in the form of a "joint and survivor" annuity, guaranteeing lifelong payments to both you and your spouse. You may take a lump sum, if available, or receive the larger payments available under an individual annuity only if both you and your spouse agree in writing to waive the joint and survivor pension.

A possible disadvantage to monthly checks is that they stop at death, even if you—or you and your spouse, under a joint and survivor arrangement—die almost immediately. There will be nothing left for your family. Meanwhile, monthly pension checks are subject to federal income tax and are taxable in the year they are received. You can arrange to have income tax withheld, or you can pay quarterly estimated taxes. One bright spot in the tax picture: Many states exclude all or part of pension income from state income tax. Pensions from careers in public service are more likely to be exempt from state income tax than pensions from the private sector.

Lump-sum distributions, on the other hand, give you a pot of cash. You can use the money to buy a retirement home, start a business, or invest for the ultimate benefit of your family. It helps, of course, if you are a wise—and lucky—investor. During boom times in the market, many retirees thought they could do better than fixed monthly payments—and wound up pinching pennies when their investments turned sour.

Lump-sum distributions are also immediately subject to income tax at ordinary income rates. If you do decide to take a lump sum, ask your employer to roll it directly into an IRA to defer tax on any portion of the account that you do not plan to use right away. When the April 1 after you reach age 70½ rolls around, you will have to start taking at least the minimum distribution required by the IRS (see below). You can withdraw more if you wish, paying tax at ordinary income rates on each distribution.

---

## PENSIONS: OUT OF STATE, OUT OF REACH

If you spent your working life in a high-tax state, you may want to find a retirement home in a state with little or no income tax. The states with no income tax—although they do have other taxes—are Alaska, Florida, Nevada, South Dakota, Texas, Washington, and Wyoming. Until 1997, such a move often failed to shelter pension income because many states (especially California and New York) aggressively went after the pension income of former residents. Today federal law prevents states from taxing the pension income of nonresidents.

---

Defined contribution plans—so called because the defined amount is your contribution rather than the expected benefit—let you choose investment vehicles for pretax contributions that will then grow tax-deferred until they are withdrawn.

If you participate in an employer-sponsored retirement plan such as a 401(k), you must start taking distributions by April 1 of the calendar year following the later of (1) the year in which you reach age 70½ and (2) the year in which you retire. When you retire, at any age, you may have several choices about how to take distributions.

- If you are not yet age 70½ (when distributions must begin), you have more than $5,000 in the account, and your employer's plan permits, you may *leave the money in place*. This is an easy solution, if you have other sources of income, and one that will keep your account growing tax-deferred. However, you may find that your investment choices are limited once you retire.

- You can take a *lump-sum distribution*, but this is usually not the best choice because you will owe income tax immediately on the entire amount. The tax is at ordinary income tax rates, currently as high as 35 percent.

- If you are at least age 59½, you may be able to take the money as an *annuity* providing a steady stream of income for life. Your employer may offer this option under the plan. If not, you can take a lump-sum distribution and use it to purchase an individual annuity. The problem with this choice is immediate taxation of the lump-sum distribution.

- The best choice, for most people, is moving all or part of the money directly into a *rollover IRA*. There are at least two good reasons for doing so. First, most company plans require the plan account to be emptied within five years of a retired employee's death; with an IRA, your beneficiaries can stretch payments over many years. Second, with a rollover IRA, you must pay income tax on any portion that you take in cash but can keep tax deferral working for you on the rest. (For more on IRA distributions, see below.)

If you have more than one defined contribution plan—such as a 401(k) plan at each of two jobs—you must take the minimum required amount from each plan once you are required to take distributions. (This is unlike IRAs—see below—where you must base your required distribution on the total in all your accounts but may take it from just one account.)

## Rollovers and Company Stock

Although rolling plan balances into an IRA is the best option for most assets, preserving tax deferral, there is one exception.

Because all assets withdrawn from an IRA are taxed at ordinary income-tax rates, rolling appreciated company stock into an IRA may lead to a large—and unnecessary—income-tax bill.

Don't worry about it if your retirement account holds a small amount of company stock. But if you hold substantial amounts of greatly appreciated company stock, as many plan participants do, it may actually save you money in the long run to take the company stock out of your tax-sheltered retirement plan when you retire and put it into a regular taxable brokerage account. You will owe ordinary income tax on the withdrawal but only on the cost basis of the stock—the price plus any transaction fees at the time the shares were acquired by the 401(k) plan—and not on the current market value.

When you sell the stock, you will owe capital-gains tax at the maximum long-term rate of 15 percent on the "net unrealized appreciation" or NUA, the gain between the original purchase by the plan and the date of withdrawal from the plan. The capital-gains rate applies to this transaction even if you sell the stock the day after the rollover. Taking advantage of NUA rules thus converts tax on the gain from ordinary income-tax rates, currently as high as 35 percent, to the lower capital-gains rate. Any additional appreciation from the date of distribution to the date of sale is taxed as either a short-term or long-term capital gain, depending on how long you have held the stock when you sell.

## Individual Retirement Accounts

As the owner of an IRA, you must begin required minimum distributions by April 1 of the year following the year in which you reach age 70½. It doesn't matter if you are still working. Unlike employer-sponsored plans such as 401(k) plans, you do not have the option of deferring distributions until you actually retire. Worse, miss a distribution and the penalty is severe—a full *50 percent* of the amount you should have taken. As CPA Ed Slott writes in *The Retirement Savings Time Bomb*, "This is one of the worst tax penalties ever conceived by Congress," one that can wipe out your retirement savings if you're not careful.

Distribution rules used to be very complicated. Fortunately, they have been simplified under new IRS regulations. There is now a single uniform life expectancy table used to calculate required minimum distributions for all IRA holders; the only exception is those whose beneficiaries are more than ten years younger. The table also permits smaller distributions than were required in the past—a boon for IRA owners who don't need the money and would like to leave it growing tax-deferred. Smaller required distributions don't limit your ability to take larger amounts if you wish to do so. (Since you pay income tax on all withdrawals, the IRS has no objection to your taking larger amounts.)

Your IRA custodian can tell you how much you must withdraw once you reach the required beginning date. You can also determine the amount by dividing your account balance at year-end by the number of years in your life expectancy (see table). The amount will change each year, along with the account balance and your life expectancy.

## Action Plan

**Step One:** Consolidate qualified plans into a single rollover IRA before your required beginning date, and the distribution calculations—along with the paperwork—will be much easier.

**Step Two:** If you have more than one IRA, you must calculate the required minimum distribution from each IRA, but you may take the required amount from just one of the accounts if you so choose. Be sure to give written notice of your intent to the financial institution holding each plan, to forestall automatic distribution.

## Action Plan

**Step Three:** Consider taking the first IRA distribution in the year in which you reach age 70½. Although you're allowed to wait until the April 1 of the following year, and may be tempted to delay so as not to pay tax on the distribution any sooner than you must, waiting means that you must take two distributions—and pay tax on both—in the same year.

## LIFE EXPECTANCY TABLE FOR IRAS

| Age | # of Years | Age | # of Years | Age | # of Years |
|-----|-----------|-----|-----------|-----|-----------|
| 70 | 27.4 | 85 | 14.8 | 100 | 6.3 |
| 71 | 26.5 | 86 | 14.1 | 101 | 5.9 |
| 72 | 25.6 | 87 | 13.4 | 102 | 5.5 |
| 73 | 24.7 | 88 | 12.7 | 103 | 5.2 |
| 74 | 23.8 | 89 | 12.0 | 104 | 4.9 |
| 75 | 22.9 | 90 | 11.4 | 105 | 4.5 |
| 76 | 22.0 | 91 | 10.8 | 106 | 4.2 |
| 77 | 21.2 | 92 | 10.2 | 107 | 3.9 |
| 78 | 20.3 | 93 | 9.6 | 108 | 3.7 |
| 79 | 19.5 | 94 | 9.1 | 109 | 3.4 |
| 80 | 18.7 | 95 | 8.6 | 110 | 3.1 |
| 81 | 17.9 | 96 | 8.1 | 111 | 2.9 |

| LIFE EXPECTANCY TABLE FOR IRAS *(continued)* | | | | | |
|------|-----------|------|-----------|-----------------|-----------|
| Age | # of Years | Age | # of Years | Age | # of Years |
| 82 | 17.1 | 97 | 7.6 | 112 | 2.6 |
| 83 | 16.3 | 98 | 7.1 | 113 | 2.4 |
| 84 | 15.5 | 99 | 6.7 | 114 | 2.1 |
|  |  |  |  | 115 and older | 1.9 |

*(Source: Internal Revenue Service)*

## Name That Beneficiary!

An IRA, like life insurance, passes directly to the beneficiary you've designated. Unlike other assets, it does not go through your will. So be sure to name both a beneficiary and a secondary (contingent) beneficiary. If you're sure you took care of this when you first opened your IRA, make sure the original designation reflects your current wishes and that the proper forms are still on file with your IRA custodian. Better yet, make out new forms, file them with your IRA custodian, and keep copies (with your other important papers) where your beneficiaries can find them. Banks and other financial institutions merge and change their names—and important documents are sometimes lost in the shuffle.

Designate a beneficiary without delay. If you fail to name a beneficiary and die before you must start taking money out at age 70½, the account will have to be paid out over five years instead of a lifetime, thereby accelerating the income tax due to Uncle Sam.

Beneficiaries may now take distributions over their own life expectancies. Your beneficiary can name a new beneficiary when the time comes, thereby stretching out the IRA distribution—

and the tax bill—over many years. For example, your 40-year-old son has a life expectancy of 43.6 years. If he dies prematurely, his beneficiary—assuming that he has named one—may continue distributions on the same schedule.

**Tax tip:** If you want your IRA split among beneficiaries, be sure to designate the share each receives. Ed Slott cites a nightmare scenario in *The Retirement Savings Time Bomb*, when a mother's wish to leave her IRA equally to her six children was circumvented by a bank's insistence that the first-named beneficiary receive it all. The only way the six sisters could honor their mother's wishes was for the oldest and first-named beneficiary to withdraw the entire amount, *pay tax on it all*, and then give her sisters their shares. Of a $600,000 IRA, more than $240,000 went to Uncle Sam in taxes. To rub salt in the wound, because our income-tax rates are graduated, the tax on the entire amount (paid by one person) was more than the combined tax on six shares (paid by six people).

## "NORMAL" RETIREMENT AGE UNDER SOCIAL SECURITY

Full Social Security retirement benefits are payable at "normal" retirement age. Until 1999, normal retirement age was always 65. Starting in 2000, it gradually increases, becoming age 67 in 2022.

| Birth Year | Normal Retirement Age |
| --- | --- |
| 1937 and earlier | 65 |
| 1938 | 65 and 2 months |
| 1939 | 65 and 4 months |
| 1940 | 65 and 6 months |
| 1941 | 65 and 8 months |
| 1942 | 65 and 10 months |

## "NORMAL" RETIREMENT AGE UNDER SOCIAL SECURITY

| Birth Year | Normal Retirement Age |
|---|---|
| 1943 through 1954 | 66 |
| 1955 | 66 and 2 months |
| 1956 | 66 and 4 months |
| 1957 | 66 and 6 months |
| 1958 | 66 and 8 months |
| 1959 | 66 and 10 months |
| 1960 and thereafter | 67 |

## Social Security

Most people think of retirement—and of Social Security retirement benefits—at age 65. But you actually have a choice. Social Security retirement benefits can start as early as age 62 or as late as age 70. Start early and benefits are permanently reduced. Since benefits may be taxable, you may want to delay payments if you have other sources of income to tide you over. Delaying payments also means larger payments—although, depending on when you die, you may never make up the lost years.

Taxation of Social Security benefits is a sore point with many retirees—especially because the money you contributed to Social Security over the years has already been taxed. Unlike contributions to tax-qualified retirement plans, FICA contributions toward Social Security and Medicare are made with after-tax dollars.

It may be double taxation, but half of the benefits are subject to income tax if you earn between $25,000 and $34,000 as a single taxpayer, or $32,000 to $44,000 as a married couple filing jointly. Fully 85 percent of benefits are subject to income tax if you earn more than $34,000 as a single taxpayer or $44,000 as a married couple filing jointly.

To add insult to injury, taxable income is given a special definition for the purpose of determining how much of your Social Security benefits are taxable: adjusted gross income (without the Social Security benefits) plus tax-exempt income (so much for tax-exempt bonds), plus half of the Social Security benefits. With this definition, not found elsewhere in the tax code, decidedly middle-income taxpayers must pay the tax. For example, a married couple with $25,000 in pension income, $18,000 of investment income, and $14,000 in Social Security retirement benefits could wind up owing an extra $1,000 in federal income tax. And, unless your state specifically exempts Social Security benefits from state income tax, you could owe state income tax on your benefits as well.

Because these threshold amounts do not change—unlike other elements of the tax code, they are not indexed to inflation—more and more Social Security recipients each year find their benefits subject to tax.

Is there anything you can do to minimize this tax? Not really, if your income is well above the threshold for taxation of Social Security benefits. Possibly yes, if your income is moderately higher than the threshold. If you don't have an immediate need for monthly pension payments, you might take your pension in a lump sum and roll it into an IRA, thereby deferring the income—and the extra income tax—until you must start IRA distributions after reaching age 70½. Another strategy, suggested by Thomas W. Batterman in the *AAII Journal*, uses a reverse approach to coordinating IRA distributions with Social Security income. If you take the minimum required amount from your IRA in the early years, in an attempt to keep taxable income down, you may wind up having to take much larger distributions in later years as the account continues to grow. Doing so could lock you into paying the highest tax on Social Security benefits as the years go by. You might be better off taking larger IRA distributions—even starting distributions before you reach the required age and before you start Social Security. The short-term pain may produce long-term gain. But each situation is different, and you should seek advice from a knowledgeable financial adviser.

## THE SOCIAL SECURITY "EARNINGS TEST"

It isn't exactly a tax, but you'll be penalized if you continue to work while receiving Social Security retirement benefits before you reach your "full" retirement age. In 2003, the full retirement age was 65 and two months for people born in 1938; it gets a little later each year until leveling out at age 67 in 2027. Sign up for Social Security before full retirement age and you can earn up to $11,250 in 2003 and keep all of your benefits; earn more, and $1 will be taken out of your Social Security check for every $2 you earn over the limit. You will also continue to pay the FICA tax for Social Security and Medicare from your earnings.

Until recently, there was an earnings test for older retirees as well. No longer. Retirees past full retirement age keep full Social Security benefits no matter how much they earn.

### Annuities

When you start to collect on an annuity, you have choices about how to take the money. The choice you make affects the tax you will pay.

If you "annuitize" the payments, taking regular payouts for life based on your individual life expectancy or the joint life expectancy of you and your spouse, each payment is made up of both principal and interest. The principal is a return of your original nondeductible contribution and is not taxed. The interest is taxed as ordinary income.

Annuitization can provide guaranteed lifetime income, but it also locks you in once the choice is made. If you take payments in the more flexible form of systematic withdrawals, the entire amount is treated as earnings (until the earnings are used up and you're tapping principal) and is therefore taxed as ordinary income. The trade-off for the flexibility of systematic withdrawals is a higher immediate tax bill—and the possibility that you may outlive your income from the annuity.

## Estate Planning to Minimize Taxes

Long-term decisions must also be made. If you haven't yet done so, now is the time to plan your estate to minimize the potential tax bite. With big changes looming in federal gift and estate taxes, getting organized now can be of enormous benefit later.

The federal tax on gifts and estates has been unified for a quarter of a century, with identical amounts excluded from tax. Under current law, the link is broken in 2004. The federal estate tax is scheduled to apply to ever-fewer people as exemptions gradually enlarge, until it disappears entirely in 2010—only to be reinstated in 2011 if Congress fails to act by then to make repeal permanent. Meanwhile, the federal gift tax will remain in effect, with a lifetime exclusion of $1 million.

## THE CHANGING FEDERAL TAX ON GIFTS AND ESTATES

| Year(s) | Exclusion Amount: Estates | Exclusion Amount: Gifts |
|---------|---------------------------|-------------------------|
| 2002–2003 | $1,000,000 | $1,000,000 |
| 2004–2005 | $1,500,000 | $1,000,000 |
| 2006–2008 | $2,000,000 | $1,000,000 |
| 2009 | $3,500,000 | $1,000,000 |
| 2010 | Estate Tax Repealed | $1,000,000 |
| 2011 | $1,000,000 | $1,000,000 |

In 2004, only estates in excess of $1.5 million are subject to federal estate tax. That sounds like—and is—a lot of money. But, before you assume that the estate tax cannot apply to you, add up the value of your home, IRA, defined contribution plan, and life insurance. You may be wealthier than you think. If so, now is the time to reduce the impact of estate tax on your family.

In this time of transition, it's important to be as flexible as possible. Most observers do not believe that the federal estate tax will be permanently repealed—but no one knows how much will be excluded from tax when the dust settles. If the exclusion remains at the $3.5 million currently scheduled for 2009, very few people will need more than a simple will. If it reverts to $1 million, many more people will have to be concerned about potential estate taxes. Meanwhile, anyone likely to have more than $1 million at death should continue tax-saving strategies for the foreseeable future.

## STATE DEATH TAXES

The federal estate tax used to include a credit for any state taxes paid on the estate. One tax thereby offset the other, so that states could reap tax revenues on the death of residents without increasing the total tax paid by the family. The 2001 law reducing and eventually eliminating the federal estate tax also did away with the offset. As a result, some states have "decoupled" their death taxes from the federal tax, some have frozen estate tax exclusions at lower levels than the federal exclusions, and some estates will pay more in total tax. You may want to look at state death taxes before you decide where to retire. It could make a big difference in the amount of tax paid by your estate.

### Where There's a Will

With or without an estate tax, everyone—old or young, married or single—should have a will. Without a will, your property will pass according to the laws of your state. With a will, you decide who will get your hard-earned property when you are gone, who will raise any minor children, and who will make sure your wishes are carried out. A will can also include tax-saving strategies such as the credit shelter trust (also called bypass trust) often used by married couples.

Married couples may leave unlimited amounts to each other, free of federal estate tax, so long as the survivor is a citizen of the United States. (If your spouse is not a citizen, you should speak with an attorney about a qualified domestic trust or QDOT.) In addition, jointly owned property passes automatically to the survivor. But this doesn't mean that you should own everything jointly—if you do, everything left by the first to die, plus growth on the assets in the intervening years, may be subject to tax on the death of the survivor. Note: In community-property states—Arizona, California, Idaho, Louisiana, Nevada, New Mexico, Texas, Washington, and Wisconsin—most property acquired during marriage is treated as if half is owned by each spouse.

## Action Plan

**Step One:** If you and your spouse have an estate potentially subject to federal estate tax, consider splitting ownership so that you each own approximately half of your assets—or, at least, up to the amount excluded from the federal estate tax. This may not be easy. While ownership of cash, securities, and most other assets can be split between husband and wife, many couples have much of their wealth tied up in their home (often best kept in joint ownership) and their retirement plans (which cannot be split). If you think estate tax may be a personal issue, talk to a knowledgeable trusts and estates attorney.

**Step Two:** Create a bypass trust in each will, allowing your surviving spouse to tap the trust if necessary but with the balance

## Action Plan

at his or her death going to your children. By passing to the children, the trust "bypasses" estate tax on the surviving spouse's death. But be careful, and get expert legal advice. Boilerplate language prior to the 2001 law often placed the full amount of the federal estate tax exclusion in trust for the children with the rest going outright to the spouse. With the exclusion rising each year for the next few years, sticking to this formula could mean leaving nothing to your spouse.

### Trusting in Trusts

The credit shelter or bypass trust is only one of many ways to shelter income from estate taxes. Other tax-saving strategies involving trusts include the following:

- Life insurance is included in your taxable estate if you own the policy. If the policy is owned by a *life insurance trust*, the proceeds will be outside your taxable estate.
- A *generation-skipping trust* shields future growth from taxes, allowing larger sums to be eventually distributed to grandchildren or great-grandchildren.
- A *qualified personal residence trust (QPRT)* similarly shields future appreciation on your home from estate tax.

Trusts are complex instruments; be sure to consult a knowledgeable attorney before deciding that one is right for you.

### Gifting

Removing assets from your estate is one way to eliminate the possibility of an estate tax on those assets. You may give up to

$11,000 each year to as many people as you like, with no gift tax obligation and no need to file a gift-tax return. You may also give as much as you like directly to an educational or medical institution on behalf of another person. And you may give up to $1 million in lifetime gifts before you must pay tax on the gift— although you must file a federal gift-tax return when gifts exceed the exemptions.

While you may give cash, giving assets likely to grow in value has the biggest bang for the buck. Giving appreciating assets, such as shares of stock, produces two tax benefits: You will no longer owe income tax on dividends, and your taxable estate is reduced by the future value of the gift.

If the recipient of your gift is a child or grandchild who is still legally a minor, you may want to establish a custodial account, trust, or college savings plan (529 plan) to hold the funds. Each has advantages and disadvantages, discussed in detail in Chapter 8. More on gifting in general is discussed in Chapter 12.

### TAX TIPS FOR JUNE

- **Estimated tax must be paid** on a quarterly basis when tax is not withheld; the second quarterly payment is due on June 15.
- **Decisions must be made** about how to take benefits from company plans, when to start Social Security, and how to take distributions from IRAs and annuities.
- **Beneficiary designations**—and not your will—determine who will receive retirement plan assets after your death.
- **If your estate may** be subject to federal estate tax, planning can minimize the impact.
- **Whether or not** your estate may be taxed, you should write a will and keep it up-to-date.

# Third Quarter: Your Life in Taxes

# CHAPTER 7

# July
## Living in a Tax Shelter

As you gather tax records for the year, don't overlook the major tax savings built into your home. In fact, over the years, your residence may provide shelter in more than one sense of the word—shelter for your family and shelter from taxes.

The U.S. tax code is an instrument of social policy, and homeownership has long been one of its primary goals. Thanks in part to all the tax breaks for homeowners, the Department of Commerce reports that at the end of 2002, 68.2 percent of Americans—81.5 percent of those aged 55 to 64—owned their own homes. With recent changes in the tax code—combined with historically low interest rates at the beginning of the twenty-first century—the number of homeowners will probably continue to increase.

This chapter deals with buying, owning, and selling your principal residence. It also describes tax issues associated with owning a second home.

## When You Buy

First a definition: Your principal residence is where you live most of the year. It is also the location where you vote, do your banking, pay taxes, register your car, and obtain your driver's license. The residence itself may be a detached house or a town house, condominium or cooperative apartment, mobile home or boat—but it must be where you live.

Most tax breaks come into play while you own your home and when you sell it. There are few tax advantages associated with the purchase itself, but there are some things you should know.

## Deductions

"Points" paid to obtain a mortgage loan are deductible if they represent prepaid interest rather than compensation for specific services such as an appraisal fee. Each point is 1 percent of the loan amount, so paying three points on a $100,000 mortgage would give you a $3,000 deduction.

You may deduct points in full in the year you buy the house or you may choose to amortize them (spread them out) over the term of the loan. If you are buying late in the year and won't have enough deductions to make it worth filing an itemized return for the year of purchase, you may be better off spreading the deduction over time. If you do so, you can take the deduction in each year of the mortgage loan. If you sell the house before you've paid off the mortgage, any balance left on the points may be taken in the year of the sale.

Another deduction available on closing is for any portion of real estate taxes you assume. If you take title on September 1 and the seller paid the third-quarter property tax on August 15, your settlement costs would normally include a proportionate share of those taxes for the number of days in the quarter that you own the house.

There is no deduction for other closing costs, although some may be added to the cost basis of the property to reduce the profit—and therefore any potential tax—that may be due when you sell. Most sellers no longer pay tax on home sales, with today's liberalized exclusions (see below), but it's worth keeping records of tax-related expenditures just in case. These items include attorney's fees, transfer taxes, title insurance and real estate commissions. They do *not* include homeowners insurance premiums, utility fees or anything else related to occupancy of the house.

---

### FINDING CASH TO BUY A HOUSE

If you have almost but not quite enough money on hand to manage a down payment on your first house, here are two possible sources of funds:

- **For the purpose of buying** your first home, you may withdraw up to $10,000 from an Individual Retirement Account without paying the 10-percent penalty normally imposed on withdrawals before age 59½. Bear in mind, though, that you will have to pay ordinary income tax on the withdrawn amount—and that you will be cutting into retirement savings.
- **If you participate** in a 401(k) plan with a loan feature, you may be able to borrow up to half of your account balance to a maximum of $50,000, or your entire balance if it is $10,000 or less. Loans to purchase a primary residence must usually be repaid within ten years, typically through payroll deduction. If you leave your job, however, you must repay the loan immediately. (For more on 401(k) plans, see Chapter 4.)

---

## While You Own

The cost of maintaining your home is never deductible. But the cost of home improvements and renovation is added to the cost basis of the house, reducing the profit when you sell and any capital-gains tax that may be due. Relatively few people owe capital-gains tax with the new home sale exclusions (see below) but you should keep records of major expenditures—a new roof, an added bathroom, and the like—just in case you fall into this elite group.

Meanwhile, you reap a host of tax advantages when you own your primary residence. The two biggest items are mortgage interest and real estate taxes.

## Mortgage Interest

Mortgage interest alone—especially in the early years, when it makes up most of each monthly payment—may put you over the top of the standard deduction, allowing you to take advantage of other itemized deductions—for state and local income tax, real estate tax, charitable contributions, and more.

Mortgage interest is fully deductible, subject to two restrictions:

1. The deductible amount is limited to interest on a mortgage of up to $1 million taken to buy, construct, or make major renovations to no more than two residences, plus interest on a home equity loan (secured by the home) of up to $100,000. Interest on larger loans is not deductible.
2. In order for the interest to be fully deductible, the mortgage cannot exceed the value of the house. As a result, taking one of the new 125-percent mortgages may mean that you cannot deduct all of the interest on the loan.

Americans tend to move long before a mortgage is paid off. If you intend to stay put, however, remember that your mortgage payment is made up largely of interest in the early years with only a pittance going toward principal. Toward the end of the mortgage term, the situation is reversed, with most of each payment going toward paying off the principal and very little in the form of deductible interest.

---

### SHORT-TERM MORTGAGES

With interest rates at all-time lows, many homeowners are taking ten-, fifteen-, or twenty-year mortgage loans—instead of the more traditional thirty-year loans—to pay off the mortgage sooner and save thousands of dollars in interest costs. A short-term mortgage may be a wise move—especially if you want to pay off your mortgage before you retire—but before you make a decision, consider:

- **your tax bracket**—the higher your bracket, the more you have to gain from making larger interest payments
- **the larger monthly payments**—and the amount of investment income you'll forgo by putting money into your mortgage instead of into another investment

---

## Real Estate Taxes

Real estate taxes are also deductible. Unlike mortgage interest—deductible on no more than two homes—property taxes may be deducted on as many homes as you own. There is no ceiling on the amount you may deduct.

If you think your real estate taxes are too high, you're not alone. You also have lots of company if you stick to grumbling instead of taking action. Even though many properties nationwide are assessed at more than their true value, according to the National Taxpayers Union, only about 2 percent of homeowners mount a challenge.

Yet filing an appeal often results in a lowered tax bill—

especially if you go about it the right way, by challenging the assessment and not the tax rate. You will never get anywhere contesting the tax rate, which is pegged to the budget process and set by law. But you can challenge the assessment on your home and land.

Before you mount a challenge, you need to understand that assessed value is not necessarily the same as market value. Sometimes it is. But your community may set assessed value at 80 percent or 40 percent—or any percentage at all—of market value. In Cook County, Illinois, for example, residential real estate is assessed at 16 percent of market value. The rate applied to the assessed value then determines the dollar amount of tax. You can challenge the assessment. You *cannot* challenge the tax rate.

The assessed value is based on your home's size, features, and characteristics. Look at the property record in your local tax assessor's office. If it says you have a fireplace when you don't or four bedrooms when you have three, it should be easy to prove your point and have your assessment reduced in a meeting with the tax assessor. On the other hand, if you recently *added* a fireplace—or an additional bedroom, a deck, or central air-conditioning—you can expect your property to be reassessed and your property taxes to go up. A Cincinnati couple's property taxes doubled, from $8,000 to $16,000 a year, when they built a horse barn and added 2,000 square feet of living space to their home.

**Tax tip:** Converting unused space to usable space—such as putting a home office in a garage or unfinished basement—typically raises property taxes less than building an addition.

If your property record is accurate, you may still be able to lower your assessment based on what similar houses have sold for in your neighborhood—although you may have to file a formal appeal and attend a hearing to do so. You can obtain recent sales prices from your local assessor's office or from a cooperative real estate agent. Other factors may also come into play, such as a utility company's right to string wires across your backyard. One New Jersey homeowner lowered her home's assessment by bringing pictures of a cracked foundation to a hearing conducted by the County Board of Assessment.

If you want to file an appeal, your local assessor's office can tell you the procedures and timetable to follow. Many assessors' offices now have Web sites with detailed information. Then, before you attend a hearing, be prepared. Consider securing an independent professional appraisal of your own property and having the appraiser accompany you to the hearing. Before the hearing, the chairman of the Arlington County (VA) Board of Equalization of Real Estate Assessments suggested in a letter to the *New York Times*, attend a meeting to see what it's like and which arguments are likely to work.

## Action Plan

**Step One:** Find out how property is assessed by your city or town.

**Step Two:** Check your property records and make sure that the information on your house is accurate. If there is an error, ask for a meeting with the local tax assessor.

**Step Three:** Find out the selling price of comparable houses in your neighborhood. If you can document that similar houses have sold for less than your assessment, or if there are other factors that reduce the value of your house, file an appeal with the local tax board or tax court.

## Casualty Losses

A "casualty," in IRS jargon, is the damage or destruction of property in a sudden, unexpected or unusual event. Gradual erosion of your home's foundation by leaking pipes is not sudden and does not qualify. Termite damage does not qualify. Damage from a hurricane, tornado, or vandalism does meet the test. Other qualifying events include fire, volcanic eruption, and sonic booms.

But casualty losses are often very difficult to deduct because the threshold is so high: $100 plus 10 percent of adjusted gross income. At an AGI of $75,000, only the uninsured portion of a loss exceeding $7,600 would be deductible.

## Action Plan

To figure out whether you have a casualty loss:

**Step One:** Look at the difference between the fair market value of your property before and after the event.

**Step Two:** Subtract any insurance on the property and an additional $100.

**Step Three:** If the resulting amount exceeds 10 percent of adjusted gross income, report the loss on Form 4684.

Note: You must file an insurance claim if the property is insured. Otherwise the casualty loss will be disallowed. What's more, if the insurance payment exceeds the amount of the loss, the difference may be treated as taxable income.

Losses due to theft are subject to the same rules—but you must prove that the item was stolen and document its value. Mysterious disappearance does not qualify as a deduction.

**Tax tip:** If a casualty loss occurs in a community designated as a "presidentially declared disaster area"—as often happens when floods or tornadoes wipe out a large region—you may deduct the loss either in the year of loss or on the prior year's tax return. For example, hurricane damage in 2004 may be deducted on your tax return for 2004 or 2003. The choice lets you receive a cash refund when you may need it most—or maximize the deduction by claiming the loss in the year when you have lower income.

## Home Sweet Cash

The equity built up in your home as you pay off your mortgage represents a major source of cash, cash that can be used to pay for life-enhancing purposes ranging from modernizing your kitchen to paying college bills for your children. You can tap the equity in your home via a home equity loan or line of credit, by refinancing or—for eligible seniors—by taking a reverse mortgage. Each course has tax implications.

### Home Equity Loans and Lines of Credit

*Home equity loans* are old-fashioned second mortgages, giving you a lump sum that must be repaid at a set date and at a fixed rate of interest. *Home equity lines of credit* are far more popular because they are far more flexible, giving you a revolving line of credit to be tapped as needed, typically by writing checks or using a special credit card. Interest on home equity lines of credit is usually variable.

Up to $100,000 in interest on home equity loans and lines of credit is fully deductible, regardless of the use to which you will put the money. But don't leap at the tax break without first assessing the entire package. Closing costs can be comparable to those on a first mortgage. Coupled with high annual fees, the total cost can outweigh the tax advantages—especially if you borrow a small amount or use a small sum from a line of credit. And—a not insignificant point—you are putting your home on the line. Because failure to repay could lead to losing your home, home equity loans should not be taken for trivial purposes.

## Refinancing

As interest rates dropped in recent years, many homeowners refinanced their mortgages—and refinanced again. If you refinance, you have several choices: You can keep the loan term the same but shrink monthly payments with a lower interest rate, freeing cash for other purposes. You can shift to a shorter-term loan, keeping monthly payments about the same but cutting years off the debt for long-term savings. You might also want to refinance for a larger sum and use the extra cash to remodel your home, repay other debts, pay college bills, or invest.

For tax purposes, if your refinancing is for the same amount as is outstanding on your original mortgage, then the mortgage is acquisition debt. If you take an additional amount—as many homeowners do—you still have acquisition debt so long as you use the money for renovations. Acquisition debt is fully deductible on loans of up to $1 million. Take out extra money and use the excess over the old loan balance for another purpose or simply to ease cash flow, however, and you will have home equity debt, deductible on loans of up to $100,000.

When you refinance an existing loan, any points on the loan cannot be deducted immediately but must be amortized over the life of the loan. Refinance a second time and you may immediately deduct the remaining points on the first refinancing.

## Reverse Mortgages

Designed for homeowners age 62 and over who own their homes with little if any outstanding debt, reverse mortgages are a way of extracting equity from a house without having to pay it back. Essentially, reverse mortgages are designed for house-rich, cash-poor older adults who need additional income. The older the borrower, in fact, the more money is available. Amounts fluctuate with interest rates but in late 2003, according to AARP, the 65-year-old owner of a house worth $200,000 could receive monthly payments of $629 under a reverse mortgage. An 85-year-old owner could receive $1,321.

A reverse mortgage is the opposite of the mortgage you take when you buy a house. The amount you can borrow is based on your age, current interest rates, and the amount of equity in your home—subject only to local caps on federally insured reverse mortgages. Income is irrelevant; you can have no income at all and still qualify for a reverse mortgage. The loan does not have to be repaid as long as you live in the house. Because no regular payments are due, there is no risk of losing the home for failure to pay. And, because the money is yours, even though it is locked into your home, it is tax-free when you take it out.

The loan must be paid off only when you die, sell your house, or move out. If the house is then worth more than the balance due on the loan (including principal, interest, and fees), your heirs can inherit the difference. If it is worth less, the lender can never collect more than the value of the home at the time of repayment. When the house is sold, in other words, the debt comes to an end—even if the sale price is less than the outstanding loan.

Reverse mortgages are very flexible. You can take the cash in regular monthly payments, in a lump sum, or as a line of credit to be tapped as needed. You can also, if you wish, combine monthly income with a line of credit. The line of credit is generally the best option—it is also the most popular—because you take only the money you need, holding the rest in reserve. Better yet, it grows over time as interest compounds on the unused balance. If you want the security of fixed monthly payments, consider adding a credit line to hedge against rising costs.

Most reverse mortgages are federally insured, with the interest rates tied to the rate on the one-year U.S. Treasury bill. Reverse mortgages are also available from a few private lenders, typically on more expensive homes and at a higher cost. Whether you go for a federally insured or private loan, pay careful attention to the associated costs. In addition to interest, you can expect to pay origination fees, closing costs, mortgage insurance, and servicing fees.

Before you decide that a reverse mortgage is right for you:

1. Read "Home Made Money: A Consumer's Guide to Reverse Mortgages," available free by calling AARP at 1-800-424-3410 (ask for publication #D15601). There is an on-line version, at www.aarp.org/revmort, with a personalized calculator to help you understand your options. Calculators are also available at the Web site of the National Reverse Mortgage Lenders Association, www.reversemortgage.org.

2. Talk to a professional counselor, available through AARP (see "Home Made Money") and through HUD's Housing Counsel Clearing House (toll-free at 1-888-466-3487). Because reverse mortgages are even more complex than ordinary mortgages, the federal government requires borrowers to receive counseling before a loan is approved. The counseling is free.

3. Discuss your decision with your family and, if you have one, an accountant or other personal financial adviser.

## When You Sell

The tax rules concerning profit on the sale of a primary residence have become blissfully simple. The only rule is that you must have owned the house for five years and occupied it for at least two of the five years. Meet this definition and, as a single taxpayer, you can exclude $250,000 of profit from your taxable income. As a married couple filing jointly, you can exclude $500,000. Even in a booming real estate market, most people will owe no tax when selling a primary residence. (Bear in mind, however, that the gain calculation includes gains on prior home sales where the tax was deferred by rolling the gain into a new house. For more information, see IRS publication #523, "Selling Your Home.")

But simple is as simple does. There are still some subtleties in the law that it pays to understand, along with some recent clarification from the IRS. Much of the news is good.

First, if you must sell before you have lived in your house for two years, you may still be able to reap some tax benefits. You qualify for a partial exclusion if you are forced to sell because of ill health, a change in job location, or "unforeseen circumstances." The latter category was a puzzlement, in the apt word of *The King and I*, until a recent IRS clarification.

Now the IRS has spelled out what it means by unforeseen circumstances. The list includes the death of the homeowner or a dependent, a natural disaster, job loss, divorce or legal separation, and multiple births resulting from the same pregnancy. Qualify under any one of these provisions, ill health, or the loss of your job, and you can exclude gain based on the number of days out of two years that you actually owned and lived in the house. As a single taxpayer living in a house for exactly one year before the sale, for example, you can enjoy gains of $125,000 free of capital-gains tax (half of the two-year period and half of the $250,000 exclusion).

In another change, unmarried joint owners may now each exclude up to $250,000 of gain on their individual share of the property.

If you run a business out of your home, you no longer need worry about allocating gain between business and residence when you sell your house, with only the gain on the residence portion excluded from tax. These complicated calculations are no longer necessary—the entire home, including the office, qualifies for the exclusion—so long as the office is within your home and not in a separate structure on your property. You must still recapture depreciation claimed on business use since May 7, 1997, at a minimum tax rate of 25 percent. (Despite the recent lowering of capital-gains tax rates, depreciation remains taxable at 25 percent. For more information on tax benefits associated with a home office, see Chapter 5.)

**Tax tip:** Although all of these new rules are effective for sales on or after December 24, 2002, the IRS has indicated that it will accept amended returns for prior years. You have three years from the original date of filing to file an amended return, or April 2005 for returns filed in April 2002 for the 2001 tax year. If you will qualify for a refund under the new rules, by all means file an amended return.

Three more notes about taxes and home sales:

- There is currently no limit on how many times the home sale exclusion may be used. Some owners of two homes have used it first on their primary residence and then on a vacation home. This is perfectly legal so long as both houses, one after the other, qualify as your primary residence and the two-years-out-of-five rule is met on each house.

- Because the cost basis on a home—a number you'll need in case tax is due—consists of the purchase price, some closing costs, and expenditures for capital improvements, you should keep track of money you spend on renovation.

- If you sell at a loss, as sometimes happens in volatile real estate markets, there is no deduction. Some homeowners, faced with a loss, convert the residence to rental property. Before taking this path, which has many tax ramifications, consult a financial adviser.

## Vacation Homes

A cabin in the woods or a cottage by the shore can be a delight for your family. It's even more delightful when you reap related tax advantages.

On the tax front, a vacation home has some similarities to a primary residence. Both mortgage interest and property taxes are deductible, although the combined mortgage loans must total no more than $1 million. Interest on home equity loans of up to $100,000 is also deductible, whether the loan is on a principal residence or a vacation home.

But there are differences as well. Points on a mortgage loan are deductible in full on a primary residence in the year you take the loan. They must be spread over the term of the mortgage loan on a second home. The biggest discrepancy, however, lies in the treatment of profit when you sell. Where gain on the sale of your primary residence may be excluded to the tune of $250,000 for single taxpayers and $500,000 for married couples filing jointly, any gain on the sale of a second home (or third, or fourth . . . ) is fully subject to tax. The tax will be at capital-gains rates, currently—thanks to the 2003 tax act—no more than 15 percent.

Use your vacation home as a source of income or to generate a tax write-off, however, and you're in a different ballpark.

A short-term rental—defined by the IRS as fewer than fifteen days in a year—doesn't affect your tax picture in any way. The rental income is not taxable and costs associated with the rental are not deductible. This is the famous "Masters" exemption, letting homeowners in Augusta, Georgia, benefit from short-term rentals during the Masters Golf Tournament.

Rent for fifteen days or more and the picture changes. In this instance, in addition to mortgage interest and property taxes, you may deduct the cost of marketing the property to potential renters along with utilities, maintenance, repairs, insurance, and depreciation. But you can't take these tax breaks if you use the house yourself for more than fourteen days or 10 percent of the number of days it is rented each year, whichever is greater. Rent out your cottage for two hundred days during the year and you can use it yourself for twenty days without disqualifying it as rental property.

Days you spend fixing up the property do not count as personal-use days, even if other family members are using the property for recreational purposes at the same time. But days lent to your in-laws do count. On the other hand, if you rent it to them at less than fair market value, you may be able to justify it to the IRS on the grounds that doing so saves on the costs of maintenance and upkeep.

And you may want to forget the whole thing and simply enjoy your vacation retreat if your adjusted gross income exceeds $100,000. Because rental income is considered "passive income" by the IRS (except when engaged in by real estate professionals), losses may be deducted only against passive gains. An exception is made for taxpayers with an AGI of up to $100,000. These taxpayers may deduct losses against ordinary income—but, even then, losses are deductible to a maximum of $25,000. The deduction phases out altogether once AGI reaches $150,000.

Mixing rental and personal use of your vacation home—renting it out for fifteen or more days and using it yourself for more than fourteen days or 10 percent of the rental period—produces what may be the most complicated tax scenario. You must report the income but you must also allocate all of your expenses between personal and business use. Rental expenses can be deducted only up to the amount of rental income, although excess amounts may be carried forward to future tax years.

## TAX TIPS FOR JULY

- **Owning a home** produces significant tax breaks, especially in deductions for mortgage interest and real estate taxes.
- **Real estate taxes** can be challenged—and often reduced—if assessments are too high.
- **Major casualty losses** may be offset with deductions.
- **Your home can produce cash** through a home equity loan or line of credit, refinancing, or—for those age 62 and older—a reverse mortgage.
- **Most homes can now be sold** without paying capital-gains tax.
- **Vacation homes yield some tax benefits,** but the tax picture is complicated if you use a vacation home to produce rental income.

# CHAPTER 8

# August
## Kids and Taxes

Children can be a bundle of joy, but there's little doubt that the bundle is expensive. Current estimates of raising a child from birth to age 18 run to about $250,000 for a two-parent family with before-tax income of about $66,000—a mind-numbing total that does not include the cost of college. Figure another $100,000 or more for four years of higher education. In the 2002–2003 school year, the College Board reported that the annual outlay for tuition and fees at a private four-year institution was $18,273. That's not the Ivy League, where tuition alone can exceed $30,000 for a single year. Nor does the figure include room and board at an average of $6,779, books, transportation, or late-night pizza.

But the cost of raising children—and especially the cost of paying for their education—can be much easier if you get organized to make the most of all the tax breaks that are available. Do so as early as possible—procrastinators lose out on years of tax-deferred and tax-free savings.

## From the Beginning

Starting with the year of birth (even if the date of birth is December 31), and lasting as long as a child is dependent on parents for support, each child provides parents with an extra personal exemption. For the 2003 tax year, each exemption reduces the family's taxable income by $3,050.

There is also a credit of $1,000 for each child under the age of 17, phasing out for parents with modified adjusted gross income over $75,000 (single) or $110,000 (married filing jointly). Unless Congress extends it at the $1,000 level, however, the credit reverts to $700 in 2005. This is another of those infamous "sunset" provisions, in which Congress gives with one hand and takes away with the other.

In addition to the exemptions and credits outlined above, parents can claim a dependent care credit (described in Chapter 1) to help defray the cost of day care and preschool incurred so that they can work outside the home. Depending on income, this credit ranges from $600 to $1,050 for one child.

If you adopt a child, up to $10,160 may be claimed as a credit for the actual expenses involved in the adoption. Qualifying expenses include adoption and attorney fees, court costs, and travel. The full credit may be claimed, even if less is spent on the adoption, if the child has special needs. The rules are slightly different for domestic and foreign adoptions, so it's important (as always!) to keep careful records of expenditures.

Again, there are phaseouts. Beginning in 2003, the phaseout of the adoption credit begins at an AGI of $152,390. The credit is eliminated at $192,390. Three other points:

- The same income limits apply to single and married taxpayers—but married taxpayers must generally file joint returns in order to claim the credit.
- It often takes more than one year to finalize an adoption. You may take the credit in each year you incur adoption-related expense, but amounts taken in one year must be deducted from the credit available in subsequent years.
- If your company benefits include reimbursement for adoption expenses, you can't also take the credit—no double

dipping allowed—but the reimbursement is not subject to income tax, although money will be withheld for Social Security and Medicare.

## Shifting Income

Moving income from your tax bracket to your child's lower bracket is a good way to reduce the tax burden for the family as a whole. If your federal income tax bracket is 28 percent or more, and your child's is 10 percent, you'll save at least 18 percent in taxes on income shifted to your child's name.

For example, if you are in the 28-percent tax bracket and own bonds paying $1,000 in annual interest, your tax on the interest will be $280. In the 10-percent bracket, your child's tax will be $100—a net saving to the family of $180. Even better, if you sell appreciated bonds after owning them for more than one year, your tax on the profit will be at the capital-gains rate of 15 percent. If your child owns the bonds, the capital-gains tax will be at 5 percent.

### The "Kiddie Tax"

But watch out for the kiddie tax. In an effort to prevent massive income shifting (and the resulting loss of tax revenue to the government), the unearned income of children under age 14 is taxed at the parent's (typically higher) marginal tax rate. Once children reach age 14, all investment income is taxed at their own rate.

But all is not doom and gloom. Children younger than 14 are not taxed at all on the first $750 they receive each year in interest or dividends and are taxed at 10 percent on the next $750. So there are still savings to be had by shifting investment income of up to $1,500 a year to each child. One way to control investment income—and the tax on that income—is to invest in growth stocks with little or no current income. Another is to purchase U.S. Savings Bonds in your child's name, deferring receipt of interest until the bonds are redeemed. (Don't elect this option if you may qualify for tax-free interest by owning the bonds yourself; see page 148.) Note: The $750 and $1,500 amounts apply to the 2003 tax year. For 2004, the figures are $800 and $1,600.

## Hire Your Kids

If you run a business, another way to shift income to your children is by putting them on the payroll. It's a win-win situation for the family: Their tax rate is lower than yours, you can deduct their salaries as a business expense, and they can start putting money away in a tax-sheltered IRA. The arrangement is completely legitimate, so long as you pay the children a reasonable wage and they actually perform real work. A 9-year-old can sweep the floor, a 12-year-old can maintain files—and a responsible teenager can answer the telephone.

The kiddie tax does not apply to earned income, so children's wages are taxed at their own rate and not yours. Better yet, earned income, unlike "unearned" or investment income, isn't taxed at all until it exceeds the standard deduction. For the 2003 tax year, the standard deduction is $4,750—for 2004, it is estimated to be $4,850—so children can earn that much tax-free. Income tax must be withheld from children's wages (they'll get a refund if earnings for the year are below the taxable amount), but FICA (Social Security) tax need not be paid on behalf of children under age 18 working for an unincorporated business owned by a parent.

## Action Plan

To lower the family tax bill:

**Step One:** Give income-producing assets to children, to reduce the income tax due on current dividends and interest as well as the capital-gains tax on sale.

**Step Two:** Because the first $750 of unearned income is tax-free and the next $750 is taxed at 10 percent, invest for growth or defer interest on U.S. Savings Bonds to keep children's annual income below $1,500 while they are under age 14 and paying taxes at the parents' rate.

**Step Three:** Put children on the payroll if you own a business; so long as they do real work, you can deduct their wages as a business expense and their earnings will be taxed at their own lower rate.

**Step Four:** Open an IRA based on children's earnings; if you wish to do so, you can make a gift to them of the contribution amount.

## Tax Returns for Children

When children under age 14 have unearned income exceeding $1,500 in 2003, a federal tax return must be filed. You have a choice. You may file a separate return for the child, using Form 8615 and attaching it to the child's Form 1040. Or you may report the child's income on your own tax return, using Form 8814 and attaching it to your Form 1040. To include the child's income on your return, that income must not exceed $7,500 and must be entirely from interest and dividends. If children have earned income or capital gains, they must file their own tax returns.

While reporting your child's investment income on your return means less paperwork—a big advantage in itself—doing so has many disadvantages. If you have more than one child, you must add up the income of all your children under age 14 and then determine how much belongs to each child. If your children have capital gains added to your income and taxed at your rate, they could wind up paying more on your return than on their own returns.

It gets worse. Adding your children's income to yours on the same tax return may produce larger adjusted gross income, thereby possibly accelerating the phaseout of itemized deductions and reducing the benefit of deductible expenses tied to income. For example, medical expenses are deductible only to the extent that they exceed 7.5 percent of AGI; if your AGI is higher because you've added in your children's income on your return, the chance of taking a deduction is smaller. You may miss out on a deductible IRA contribution if your child's income pushes you over the ceiling. Both the child tax credits and the child-care credit may be reduced. And, if you live in a high-tax state pegging its income tax to the federal tax, you'll pay more in combined federal-state taxes.

## College Savings

The two most expensive purchases most people make are the family home and a college education for the children. At $25,000-plus for one year of college—and with college costs escalating beyond the rate of inflation for the last several years—it's almost impossible for today's young people to work their way through college. Part-time and summer earnings can defray some of the cost, providing spending money if little more, but annual tuition costs are just too high for even the most hardworking students to cover on their own.

The financial aid available from colleges has also been curtailed in days of budget crunch. That leaves the job to parents. Fortunately, there are a number of tax breaks to ease the pain between birth and the freshman year.

## Long-term Savings

Getting started early is the key to painless saving—and to reaping tax benefits year after year. There are several college savings vehicles blessed by Uncle Sam with tax advantages. They vary in the amount that may be contributed, how the money may be used, and the specific tax benefits. One or more may be right for you, but compare carefully before you decide.

**Custodial Accounts.** For many years, custodial accounts under the Uniform Gifts to Minors Act (UGMA) or the Uniform Transfers to Minors Act (UTMA) were virtually the only game in town for college savings. Custodial accounts are still available, but there are a host of other options, many of them far superior in offering tax deductions and tax deferral.

However, you may want to use a custodial account, either alone or in tandem with another vehicle—one advantage is that assets in a custodial account belong to the child and are therefore out of your taxable estate—so here are the ground rules.

It's easy to establish a custodial account at most financial institutions. There are no income ceilings and the amount you can put away is limited only by the $11,000-per-person-per-year exclusion from gift tax. Cash and securities are most often used to fund custodial accounts. In states with the more inclusive Uniform Transfers to Minors Act, insurance policies and real estate may also be used.

There is no deduction for gifts to a custodial account, and growth in the accounts is not tax-deferred. Annual investment income in excess of $1,500 is subject to tax, at the parents' tax rate for children under age 14 and at the child's (presumably lower) tax rate at 14 and over.

You control the way the money is invested—but the money belongs to the child. You can tap the account only for the child's benefit—and, even then, since the IRS expects you to provide routine support, any withdrawals will probably have to go for "extras" such as summer camp. Worse, the child has full access to the account at legal age (18, in most states) and will then have complete discretion as to how the money is used. You won't have much to say—put another way, they may not listen—if Junior or Suzie decides to run off with a rock band or buy a red sports car instead of going to college.

**Tax tip:** If you open a custodial account, name yourself as custodian, and die before the child reaches legal age, the money will be back in your (potentially taxable) estate. You can avoid this outcome by naming a trusted relative as custodian in your place.

Money in the child's name may also put a real damper on chances for financial aid. The financial aid formula assumes that 35 percent of the money in a child's name is available to pay college bills, against only 5.6 percent of assets owned by parents. If you expect your child to qualify for financial aid, a custodial account may not be a good choice.

If assets in a student's name earn enough income (once the child reaches age 19, with or without his or her own earnings) to provide more than half of the student's support for the year, you lose the student as a dependent on your federal income-tax return.

**Coverdell Education Savings Accounts.** Originally known as "education IRAs," although they never had anything to do with retirement, Coverdell accounts let you save up to $2,000 per child per year in a tax-deferred savings account. Contributions are not deductible, but earnings are not taxed during the accumulation period. They are taxed at withdrawal—and subject to a 10 percent tax penalty if the money is not used for educational expenses.

A big plus for Coverdell accounts: They are not currently limited to funding higher education. Until the end of 2010, later if extended by Congress, money may be withdrawn for expenses associated with elementary and secondary education, including tutoring and after-school programs.

But there are income limitations. Contributions are reduced if your modified adjusted gross income exceeds $95,000 for a single taxpayer or $190,000 for a married couple filing jointly. They are eliminated altogether for single taxpayers at $110,000 and married taxpayers at $220,000.

Two other drawbacks: Money not spent on college expenses must be given to the child, although money designated for a child who chooses not to attend college may be rolled over to an account for another child. And a Coverdell account, like a custodial account, is treated as the child's asset and can therefore hamper eligibility for financial aid.

**United States Savings Bonds.** Interest on Series EE and I bonds issued after December 31, 1989, can be tax-free when used for college expenses if certain conditions are met:

- The owner of the bonds must be at least age 24, which means that the bonds cannot be owned by the child.
- Proceeds must be used for tuition and fees—not room, board, or books—and are tax-free only if the principal plus interest on the redeemed bonds does not exceed actual expenses in the year they are redeemed. This is important: Do not redeem bonds if their combined principal and interest exceed tuition and fees for the year.
- Income must be under specified limits in the year the bonds are redeemed. For 2003 (amounts change each year), the phaseout ranges are $58,500 to $73,500 for single taxpayers and $87,750 to $117,750 for married taxpayers filing jointly. Taxpayers whose filing status is "married filing separately" may not take advantage of this tax break.

Savings bonds have some advantages: They can be purchased for as little as $25 at most banks and at $100 through payroll-deduction programs at many companies. There are no commissions or fees attached to the purchase. Bond proceeds can be used anywhere, at any college or university. Bond proceeds may also be used to make contributions to a Coverdell Education Savings Account or a qualified tuition program (see below). If the proceeds are not used for education, income tax will be due on the interest, but there is no tax penalty.

If you purchase savings bonds as part of your college savings plan, be sure to keep good records. Daniel J. Pederson, author of *Savings Bonds*, suggests that your records on each bond include the Social Security number of the owner, serial number, face value, issue date, date of redemption, and total proceeds. The IRS will also want to know the name of the educational institution receiving payment, the date the expenses were paid, and the amount of qualified expenses. Forms 8815 and 8818 may be used for this purpose.

**Qualified Tuition Programs (QTPs).** These enormously popular plans, grouped under the name "529 plans" for the authorizing section of the Internal Revenue Code, have many advantages. Contributions are not deductible on your federal tax return, although some states offer tax breaks to residents using state plans. But contributions grow tax-deferred and earnings are completely tax-free if used for tuition, fees, books, or room and board—although this provision will "sunset" in 2010 unless Congress enacts legislation to extend the tax-free status of withdrawals. Parents and grandparents at any income level may make contributions. Those contributions are limited in amount only by state ceilings on anticipated educational costs. Some states allow contributions of up to $300,000 or so on behalf of a single beneficiary.

As a practical matter, annual contributions are generally limited by the annual federal gift-tax exclusion ($11,000 in 2003)—except that 529 plans come with a special bonus. You may make five years' worth of gifts at one time—up to $55,000 per person, $110,000 for a married couple—with no gift-tax obligation. If you have this kind of money to put toward the future education of a child or grandchild, you can really jump-start college savings. If you give the full amount, however, you may not give that same child any additional gifts for the next four years. A birthday trinket may pass unnoticed, but steer clear of birthday checks that push you over the top.

In another significant advantage for upper-bracket taxpayers, contributions to 529 plans are considered a "completed gift," unlike any other gift where the giver retains control. In other words, you get to choose the investments in the plan from the menu offered by the provider. You can even change the beneficiary to another member of your family. Yet the contribution, once made, is out of your estate. For grandparents with sizable estates that may be subject to federal estate tax, this can be an ideal strategy for removing assets from the estate while helping grandchildren receive an education.

## A GENERATION GAP

One of the major advantages of qualified tuition programs is that you can change the beneficiary. There is no income tax payable so long as the new beneficiary is a member of the original beneficiary's family. Skip a generation, however—shifting beneficiaries from your child to a grandchild, as an example—and the original beneficiary will owe gift tax on the transfer. Skip two generations, and a generation-skipping tax may also come into play.

QTPs come in two varieties: prepaid tuition plans and college savings plans.

**Prepaid tuition plans,** allowing you to purchase part or all of tomorrow's tuition at today's prices, are offered by many states and by many individual private institutions as well. An umbrella prepaid program announced in early 2003, the Independent 529 Plan, includes about three hundred universities.

The guarantee appeals to many parents, but Joseph F. Hurley, author of *The Best Way to Save for College* and founder of www.savingforcollege.com, a Web site evaluating 529 plans, points to several possible disadvantages:

- There are often restricted enrollment periods.
- Most state-run prepaid programs require that either the donor or the beneficiary live in the state.
- Many programs cover only tuition and fees, not room and board or other expenses of higher education.
- Financial aid eligibility is reduced by the prepaid tuition.

Moreover, some states do not guarantee that prepayments will cover tuition. With escalating college costs and diminishing stock market returns for state investment pools, some states have been forced to sharply increase the price of prepaid tuition. From September 2001 to January 2003, for example, the purchase price for one year of prepaid tuition in Ohio's plan jumped from $5,100 to $8,150.

**College savings plans** are far more flexible than prepaid tuition plans. Sponsored by the states and typically run by an investment manager (some of the best-known mutual fund families are among the investment managers), these plans let you invest money toward future college costs. Most states make their plans available to residents of other states (although state income-tax benefits, where available, go only to residents of the offering state). Most plans offer a choice of investment tracks. Better yet, the proceeds can be used anywhere. You do not have to limit your child's future choices to a specific school or state.

529 plans are so flexible, in fact, that you can even name yourself as the beneficiary. Joseph Hurley suggests that this strategy might come into play if you have already made gifts this year to a child or grandchild and don't want to exceed the annual gift

exclusion. Start the plan, name yourself as beneficiary, then re-place yourself with the child as beneficiary in a later year when the gift-tax exclusion is again available. You might even do the same in advance of having children or grandchildren. The pro-ceeds will be tax-free if you decide to pursue higher education. If not, when a child or grandchild does arrive on the scene, you can simply change the beneficiary.

Two developments—recent stock market declines and the lower tax rate for dividends enacted in 2003—have combined to make some people question the wisdom of investing in college savings plans. Instead, to retain the flexibility of using the money for other purposes, you might want to consider investing in a solid growth-and-income fund or specific growth stocks, paying the minimal tax on dividends (see Chapter 9.) The jury is still out but, for some parents, 529 plans will continue to have one significant advantage: If you have a potentially taxable es-tate, 529 plans will continue to offer unparalleled advantages, letting you remove large amounts from the estate while retaining control over the assets.

## MAKING A SWITCH

Not happy with investment performance in your 529 plan? Finding that fees are growing unreasonably? Federal law al-lows you to move funds once a year from one sponsored plan to another. In fact, according to PricewaterhouseCoopers' *Guide to the New Tax Rules*, "The rollover option allows trans-fers between the tuition plans of different states, between a state's prepaid tuition plan and its savings plan, or between a state tuition plan and a private plan." But plans are not required to permit rollovers—and many states are making transfers tax-able—so this is something to check before you sign on the dot-ted line.

---

## MAKING A SWITCH

Want to switch funds from a custodial account to a 529 plan? You may do so—but, since contributions to a 529 plan must be made in cash, you will first have to liquidate assets in the custodial account (possibly incurring taxes) and then invest in the 529.

---

# Here and Now

As college looms on the horizon, financial aid becomes important for many families. Here is where college savings in your child's name may hurt rather than help. So may rising home equity where colleges count it in the formula for assessing need. The federal aid formula does not consider the value of your home, but many colleges do. The good news is that some colleges have begun to cap the amount of home equity considered as available for education. Still, just to be on the safe side, you may want to take a home equity loan or line of credit while your youngster is still in high school. Doing so reduces the amount of equity in your home theoretically available to pay for college.

Once children enter their freshman year, most parents feel the die is cast—it's too late to do much in the way of saving. That's not quite true—at least three years of tuition bills remain to be paid after freshman year. Even in senior year, there are a number of tax-saving strategies that can ease the burden via credits and deductions.

Credits are more valuable than deductions. Credits represent a dollar-for-dollar tax saving. Deductions are as valuable as your marginal tax rate; if you are in the 28-percent tax bracket, each deduction produces a saving of $28 for every $100 spent.

## Education Credits

There are two education tax credits, both applicable to tuition and fees. Both are claimed on Form 8863. Both phase out at an adjusted gross income of $40,000 to $50,000 for single taxpayers, $80,000 to $100,000 for married couples filing jointly. But only one of the credits may be taken in the same year for the same student; neither can be claimed if you take a deduction for tuition (see below) for the same student. And you cannot claim either education credit if you file your tax return as married filing separately.

- The Hope scholarship credit provides up to $1,500 in tax credits, per student per year, but only for the first two years of college. The credit is 100 percent of the first $1,000 of tuition payments and 50 percent of the next $1,000, both figures adjusted annually for inflation.
- The Lifetime Learning credit is per-family, not per-student, and provides a credit up to $2,000 a year. The credit is calculated as 20 percent of up to $10,000 in tuition and fees.

## COMPARING EDUCATION CREDITS

| Benefit | Hope Scholarship Credit | Lifetime Learning Credit |
|---|---|---|
| Annual amount | Up to $1,500 per student | Up to $2,000 per family |
| Availability | First two years of undergraduate study | All undergraduate and graduate study for an unlimited number of years |
| Limitations | Student must be enrolled at least half-time in a degree program | Can be claimed for one or more courses, whether or not student is pursuing a degree |

## Education Deductions

Two deductions related to higher education have recently been added to the tax code. Both are "above the line" deductions and can be claimed even if you take the standard deduction. Again, neither can be claimed if your filing status is married filing separately.

1) Through the end of 2005, there is a deduction for tuition payments. For 2003, taxpayers with an adjusted gross income of not more than $65,000 (single) or $130,000 (married filing jointly) may deduct up to $3,000 of tuition and fees; at higher incomes there is no deduction. The picture gets brighter in 2004 and 2005. Then, subject to the same income limits, the deduction is up to $4,000 of tuition and fees. But higher-income taxpayers benefit as well—in these two years alone, taxpayers with an AGI up to $80,000 (single) and $160,000 (married filing jointly) may deduct up to $2,000 of tuition and fees. You may not take the deduction for tuition payments and also claim one of the education tax credits.

2) Up to $2,500 in interest on college loans may be deducted, whether or not you itemize deductions on your federal income-tax return. The deductible amount is reduced for taxpayers with an AGI of more than $50,000 (single) or $100,000 (married filing jointly), with the income limitation adjusted annually for inflation.

If your income is too high to qualify for these deductions, consider having the student make the tuition payments and take out the loans. You will not be able to claim the student as your dependent if he or she takes the deduction, but the deduction may be worth more than the dependency exemption. In any case, when it comes to a loan, the child is not likely to be your dependent after graduation, when repayment begins.

## IRAS FOR EDUCATION

Still short of cash for college bills? You can withdraw money from an IRA, without penalty, to pay qualified educational costs. However, you will owe income tax on the withdrawal—and this strategy should be a last resort, because it will harm your own savings for retirement.

### Juggling Act

Tax breaks for education are among the most complicated to apply, and making a mistake can be costly. Using some benefits precludes using others. Moreover, the ones you can use must be taken in sequence, and in no case can you claim credits, deductions, or exclusions for more than the amount of qualified education expense incurred in a given year. As John W. Roth, a federal tax analyst for tax publishers CCH, notes, "There's a general rule against double-dipping. Taking one tax credit, for example, often means that you lose another credit, deduction or exclusion. You want to make sure you choose the provisions that do you the most good."

To some extent, this situation has improved. Before 2002, using proceeds from a Coverdell account precluded claiming the Hope or Lifetime Learning credit. Now—at least until the act "sunsets" on December 31, 2010—you may use a Coverdell and also claim one of the education credits so long as the money is not applied to the same expenses. You don't have to take a tax credit but, if you do, it comes first. And you don't have to take withdrawals from Coverdell accounts or college savings plans but, if you do, says Mr. Roth, you must do so before you can cash out U.S. savings bonds and exclude the interest income.

## Action Plan

To make college costs manageable:

**Step One:** Take out a home equity loan or line of credit during your youngster's high school years to reduce the equity in your home that colleges may otherwise consider available to pay tuition.

**Step Two:** Apply for direct scholarships and grants to reduce the cost of tuition.

**Step Three:** Claim either the Hope or Lifetime Learning credit if your income is below $40,000 to $50,000 (single) or $80,000 to $100,000 (married filing jointly).

**Step Four:** If you have saved money toward college in a Coverdell Education Savings Account or Qualified Tuition Program, exclude these amounts.

**Step Five:** Reduce any remaining tuition by qualified savings bond interest if you meet income limitations.

**Step Six:** Ease the remaining tuition burden by claiming a tax deduction for tuition payments and (if you meet income limitations) a tax deduction for up to $2,500 in interest on college loans.

## TAX TIPS FOR AUGUST

- **You may claim a personal exemption** for each dependent child and, if income requirements are met, a child tax credit of $1,000 for each child under the age of 17.
- **Shifting income to children** by putting income-producing assets in their name—and, if you own an unincorporated busi-

## TAX TIPS FOR AUGUST

ness, by paying them wages for real work—can reduce the overall family tax burden.

- **Long-term college savings** that produce tax benefits include Coverdell Education Savings Accounts, U.S. Savings Bonds, and the Qualified Tuition Programs known as 529 plans.
- **The Hope and Lifetime Learning credits** can reduce the family tax bill while children are in college.
- **Deductions can be claimed** for tuition payments and for some of the interest on college loans.

# CHAPTER 9

# September
# Investment Wins and Losses

As an investor, you seek current income, future growth, or some combination of the two. Since taxes can have a substantial impact on both current income *and* future growth, investing without an eye to tax consequences is nothing short of foolhardy. And putting off consideration of the tax consequences until you sell can produce a procrastinator's worst nightmare.

With the exception of investments held in tax-deferred accounts such as IRAs and 401(k) plans, most investments are subject to tax on income (dividends and interest) while you hold them and on profits (even on otherwise tax-exempt securities) when you sell. For many years, dividends and interest were taxed as current income, while profits on the sale of securities held for more than one year were taxed at lower capital-gains rates. But the far-reaching law enacted in 2003 dramatically changed the tax on both income and gains—at least temporarily. As is the case with so much in recent tax law, the provisions "sunset" at the end of 2008. In 2009, unless Congress acts to extend the current rates, all rates revert to pre-2003 levels.

## Investment Income

Interest and dividends have long been taxed as ordinary income—if you paid Uncle Sam 25 percent of your salary in income tax, you paid the same 25 percent on interest and dividends. In 2002, when the highest tax rate on ordinary income stood at 38.6 percent, so did the tax on investment income in the form of interest and dividends.

In 2003, the rules changed. Interest is still taxed at ordinary income rates—although all tax rates have been reduced retroactive to January 1, 2003, with the current top rate at 35 percent. But most dividends are now taxed at a maximum rate of 15 percent. As a result, there is now a 20-percent spread between the top tax rate of 35 percent on income, including interest income, and the top tax rate of 15 percent on dividends. For taxpayers in the higher brackets, the difference is significant. Under prior law, Joe Smith sees an after-tax return of $650 on every $1,000 of dividend income after paying income tax at the top rate of 35 percent. Under the new 15-percent rate schedule, he pockets $850 on the same dividend income.

But nothing is simple in the world of tax law. For purposes of the lower rate, there are "qualifying" and "nonqualifying" dividends. The ordinary income-tax rate still applies to nonqualifying dividends, a category that includes dividends on any stock owned for less than sixty days, stock issued by some foreign corporations, and most shares of real estate investment trusts (REITs). Special rules also apply to mutual funds, as described below.

### Mutual Fund Dividends

Funds call their distributions dividends—but some of the distributions are based on dividends from stocks held in the funds while others are based on interest income from bonds. The two are now treated differently for tax purposes and will have to be properly labeled by the funds in their year-end information returns. Check those 1099 forms carefully!

Qualified dividends received by mutual funds and passed through to shareholders are now taxed at no more than 15 percent. Shareholders in bond funds and money market funds, however, will pay income tax at ordinary rates on the interest passed through on those investments. Shareholders in some types of funds—such as balanced funds, containing both stocks and bonds, and income funds where income is based on interest as well as stock dividends—will have to pay close attention to year-end mutual fund statements detailing income categories for tax purposes.

Other rules relating to mutual fund taxation remain the same under the 2003 law. Both interest and dividends are taxable in the year they are paid by the company. It makes no difference to Uncle Sam whether you take distributions in cash or reinvest them to purchase additional shares. Distributions of both interest and dividends are included in the 1099 form you receive from the mutual fund and must be included in your taxable income.

## Capital Gains

The 2003 law, reducing the maximum long-term capital-gains tax to 15 percent, also has a significant impact on investors.

The basic distinction is between short-term gains and long-term gains:

- Sell securities held for one year or less (defined as "short-term") and any profit is taxed at ordinary income rates as high as 35 percent.

- Gains on securities held for more than one year ("long-term") are now taxed at the maximum capital-gains rate of 15 percent (see table), except that taxpayers in the 10-percent and 15-percent tax brackets pay no more than 5 percent on long-term gains. The 15-percent rate "sunsets" at the end of 2008, returning to the pre-2003 maximum rate of 20 percent. The 5-percent rate drops to zero for 2008 and then, unless Congress takes action to extend the lower rates of the 2003 law, it also returns to prior rates.

## SHORT-TERM AND LONG-TERM GAINS

| Tax Rate | Short-term Gains | Long-term Gains |
|----------|------------------|-----------------|
| 10% | 10% | 5% |
| 15% | 15% | 5% |
| 25% | 25% | 15% |
| 28% | 28% | 15% |
| 33% | 33% | 15% |
| 35% | 35% | 15% |

Note: These new lower rates do not apply to sales of collectibles or to recaptured depreciation on real estate. If you sell your collection of Beanie Babies at a profit, the tax on that profit is still 28 percent. If you sell your house after claiming depreciation on a home office, that depreciation is "recaptured" (meaning that it is currently taxable) at 25 percent. These rates have not changed. Also, while investment losses may offset investment gains (see page 170), you reap no tax benefit from losses on personal property. If you lose money on the sale of your Beanie Babies collection or your house, you cannot use the loss to reduce the taxes you owe.

Unlike the reduction of the tax rate on dividend income, which was made retroactive to January 1, 2003, the lowered capital-gains rate was effective midyear, on May 6, 2003. Since different tax rates apply, depending on when gains were realized, calculations on gains will be more complicated for the 2003 tax year. In fact, the IRS estimates that up to 6 million taxpayers who could file Form 1040A when reporting capital-gains distributions in prior years will now have to file Form 1040 and attach Schedule D, "Capital Gains and Losses."

In general, gain is determined by comparing the sales price with the cost basis. The cost basis is the original purchase price plus any transaction costs, such as fees and commissions. If you receive securities as a gift—from doting parents, as an example— your gain, if any, is determined by comparing your sales price to their original cost basis. If you inherit securities, however, your cost basis is determined at the date of the original owner's death. This provision—known as a "step-up" in basis—can serve to greatly reduce tax otherwise due on the sale of securities that have appreciated for decades. (Under current rules relating to inherited assets, the "step-up" rule will be eliminated if the federal estate tax is repealed as scheduled in 2010.)

For example, let's say Jackie sells shares of stock for $20,000. The shares were originally purchased by her mother and have a cost basis of $10,000. Jackie could owe very different amounts of capital-gains tax, depending on how she acquired the shares:

- If the shares were a gift from her mother, she owes capital-gains tax on the full $10,000 in profit. At the 15-percent rate on long-term gains, the tax bill is $1,500.
- If the shares were inherited from her mother and were valued at $18,000 at the time of her mother's death, Jackie enjoys $8,000 of appreciation without tax. She owes 15 percent of only the $2,000 in subsequent appreciation, or $300.

With the significant spread between the tax on short-term property at ordinary income rates and the new lower tax rate on long-term property, it may pay to hold on to investments until you qualify for the lower capital-gains tax rates. But taxes should never be the tail that wags the investment dog. Take the tax burden into account, by all means, but also weigh prospects for the investment before you decide whether to sell or hold.

## Mutual Fund Gains

There are two types of capital gains attributable to mutual funds, one taxed while you own your shares and the other when you sell.

*While you own shares,* you pay tax each year on capital-gains distributions based on transactions within the fund. These distributions, typically declared late each year, have nothing to do with whether or not you personally sold any shares. Equally important, capital-gains distributions, along with interest and dividends, are taxed each year *even if you reinvested them to buy additional shares and did not take them in cash*. Legislation introduced in Congress in 2003, but not passed into law at this writing, would allow mutual fund shareholders to defer taxes on reinvested capital gains until fund shares are sold.

Meanwhile, you may owe tax on year-end capital-gains distributions from a mutual fund *even if the fund lost money for the year*. Capital-gains distributions are based on transactions within the fund portfolio—and a manager may sell a stock that is down 20 percent for the year but up 40 percent since it was purchased by the fund. The result: You pay tax on profit you never see.

*When you sell mutual fund shares,* the sales are subject to the same capital-gains tax rules as other investments. If you sell all of your shares at one time, the tax on any profit is based on the difference between the sales price and your cost basis. But sales of fund shares become far more complicated when (1) you reinvested dividends and therefore bought additional shares at varying prices and (2) you sell part but not all of your holdings at one time.

Buying shares at regular intervals is a terrific way to "dollar cost average," to buy more shares when prices are down and fewer when prices are up. When you reinvest dividends to buy more shares, you typically end up with more shares at a lower average price. Invest regularly and you can smooth market fluctuations by reducing the average cost of share purchases over time (see table). Dollar cost averaging does not guarantee a profit or prevent a loss if share prices continue to decline over time, but it does tend to minimize risk for long-term investors.

## DOLLAR COST AVERAGING

| Amount Invested | Number of Shares Purchased | Share Price |
| --- | --- | --- |
| $100 | 10 | $10.00 |
| $100 | 20 | $ 5.00 |
| $100 | 10 | $10.00 |
| Total: $300 | Total: 40 | Average: $ 7.50 |
| Average share cost ($300 divided by 40 shares) = $7.50 | | |

But reinvested dividends are tricky because, without proper records, you will wind up paying tax twice on the same money. Because you paid taxes on the dividends when received (even when you reinvested those dividends), you do not owe tax again on the same money when the shares purchased with those dividends are sold. Instead, you should add the cost of those shares to the cost basis of the shares you already own. If you procrastinate, if you wait until you sell to figure out the adjusted cost basis, you will have an impossible task—unless you have kept meticulous records along the way. (If you're desperate at the time of sale, ask your mutual fund; some funds will give you a record of your transactions—although, as we'll see below, their records may not support the lowest tax cost.)

Making a mistake in calculating cost basis can be very expensive. Look what happened to Eric. Years ago he bought five hundred shares in a mutual fund for $10,000. Over the years he invested another $10,000 in the form of dividends and capital-gains distributions. When he sold his entire position in the fund for $40,000, he reported a $30,000 capital gain (the $40,000 sales price minus the original $10,000 purchase price). But he forgot about the reinvested dividends—the $10,000 on which he had already paid tax. His actual gain was $20,000 and he paid capital-gains tax on $10,000 more than necessary. At the long-term capital-gains rate of 15 percent, the overpayment was $1,500.

Calculating taxes accurately becomes even more complex if you sell—as many investors do—a portion of your fund shares rather than all the shares you own. The IRS gives you a choice when it comes to reporting gains on sales of partial holdings. The choice you make can have an enormous impact on how much tax you pay—but the choice you *can* make is dictated by the kind of records you keep along the way. If you procrastinate about getting your records in order, records that can document your cost basis on each share purchase, you may pay a lot more tax than you should.

There are four choices. Before you throw up your hands at the complexity the choices represent, know that the choice you make really does make a difference in the amount of tax you pay. In the following example from the Investment Company Institute, taxable gains on the same sale could range from as little as $200 to as much as $1,500. Let's say you purchased one hundred shares of the XYZ mutual fund in January 1998 at $20 a share, one hundred shares in January 1999 at $30 a share, and one hundred shares in April 2002 at $46 a share. Your total cost was $9,600. You sold fifty shares in March 2003 for $50 a share. I'll explain how each choice works, then show how much tax would be due.

**First-in-first-out (FIFO).** This is the easiest selection because it assumes that the first shares purchased are the first shares sold. It also tends to be the most expensive in terms of the tax you pay. Because it often produces the largest capital-gains tax—the longer you have held shares, the more likely they are to have appreciated in price—it is also the method that the IRS will assume you are using unless you specify a different choice.

Using the first-in-first-out method, your cost basis per share is $20, producing a taxable capital gain of $1,500 (the $2,500 sales price minus the $1,000 purchase price of the original fifty shares). This is the largest tax bite on this particular transaction. While it doesn't always produce the largest tax bill, FIFO produces the lowest capital gain only when a fund has consistently lost money and the share value at the time of the sale is below your purchase price.

**Specific identification.** If you keep detailed records of every share purchase, you can reduce the tax bite by selling the shares with the highest cost basis. To do so, you must write a letter to the mutual fund or stockbroker, identifying the specific shares you're selling by their purchase date and price. The fund or broker must then provide written confirmation of your instructions.

Under the specific identification method, you would naturally sell the shares bought most recently because they have the highest purchase price. With a cost basis of $46 per share, you have a capital gain of $200.

**Average cost.** Under this method, you determine the average cost for each of your shares by adding up their total cost and then dividing by the number of shares. Average cost is the method used by most mutual fund companies who provide cost basis information to shareholders, but it may not produce the best results. In addition, once you select the average cost method with respect to a particular fund, you must continue to use this method on future sales from the same fund unless you receive IRS approval to make a change.

Using the average cost method for all of your shares, your cost basis per share is $32 (your total $9,600 purchase price divided by the three hundred shares you now own). This gives you a capital gain of $900 (the $2,500 sales price minus an average purchase price of $1,600).

**Average cost "double-category"** is a variation on the average cost theme, in which you first divide your shareholdings into two groups, those held short-term (twelve months or less) and those held long-term (more than twelve months), and derive the average cost for each group. If you choose this method, you must notify your mutual fund or broker which category represents the shares you intend to sell.

With average cost, double category, you own two hundred shares at a total purchase price of $5,000 for an average cost of $25 per share, and one hundred shares at $4,600 for an average cost of $46 per share. Your taxable gain using the long-term shares would be $1,250 (taxed at the capital-gains rate) while your taxable gain using the short-term shares would be $200 (taxed at your rate for ordinary income, a maximum of 35 percent). If you do not specify which category of shares you are selling, the IRS will assume that you are selling the long-term shares.

Mutual funds in which you own shares will send you a breakdown each year of taxable and tax-exempt income. Note, though, that some seemingly tax-exempt income becomes taxable under certain circumstances. You may owe taxes on "tax-free" funds if:

- You own shares in a fund holding municipal bonds issued by many states or by a single state other than the one in which you live. Municipal bonds are generally tax-free when it comes to federal income tax but are free of state income tax only to residents of the issuing state.
- You own shares in a fund holding so-called "private activity bonds"—municipal bonds issued to support such pur-

poses as building a convention center or sports arena—
and are subject to the alternative minimum tax (discussed
in Chapter 12).

---

## FOUR MUTUAL FUND TAX TRAPS

- **Fund "families" make** it easy to exchange shares of one fund for shares of another. But easy doesn't mean tax-free. With the exception of money market mutual funds, an exchange is a sale of shares in one fund and a purchase of shares in another. You may owe tax on the sale.
- **Some mutual funds** advertise that they can be used as substitutes for a checking account. With the exception of money market mutual funds, where the net asset value generally remains at $1, writing a check sells shares and is therefore a taxable event.
- **Some mutual funds** advertise themselves as tax-free because their portfolios hold tax-free municipal bonds. Even if the interest on the bonds is totally tax-free (not always the case), gain on the sale of these funds is always taxable.
- **Mutual funds** are required by law to distribute most of their income to shareholders each year. They typically do so in December. If you buy shares right before the distribution date, you will pay tax on the distribution but derive no benefit because the share price generally falls to reflect the distribution.

---

## Investment Losses

Capital gains are taxed at preferable rates—but what if you have losses instead of gains? If your investment portfolio heads south, as it did for many investors during the bear market of the last few years, you are not alone. If you sold those investments and suffered an actual loss—not solely a paper loss—you may be able to use the tax law to offset some of your grief.

If you have taken gains as well as losses, you can write one off against the other to eliminate some or all of the tax you would otherwise pay on the gain. If net losses exceed net gains, you may deduct up to $3,000 of losses against ordinary income. The amount has remained static for decades, despite recent discussion in Congress about increasing it to a more reasonable level. The amount applies to both single taxpayers and married couples filing jointly. Married couples filing separately may each deduct up to $1,500 in capital losses.

If the $3,000 doesn't cover your losses, you may carry them forward indefinitely to future years. In each year, you may apply the carried-forward losses to offset gains, or deduct the excess—again, up to $3,000—against ordinary income. As you go forward, short-term losses are first applied to offset any short-term gains in the carryover year, while long-term losses first offset long-term gains. Each type of loss may then be applied against the other and, lastly, against ordinary income. For example: George Gibson has $1,100 in net short-term capital loss and $2,800 in net long-term capital loss for the year, for a total loss of $3,900. He may apply the full $1,100 in short-term loss and $1,900 of the long-term loss to offset $3,000 of ordinary income. The remaining $900 of net long-term capital loss is carried over to the following year.

## Action Plan

**Step One:** Determine whether you sold securities that have been held short-term (twelve months or less) or long-term (more than twelve months).

**Step Two:** Add all your short-term capital gains for the year and then subtract all of your short-term capital losses.

## Action Plan

**Step Three:** Add your long-term gains and subtract any long-term losses.

**Step Four:** If net losses (short-term and long-term) exceed net gains (short-term and long-term), deduct up to $3,000 of losses (short-term losses first) against ordinary income.

**Step Five:** Carry forward any loss in excess of $3,000 to future years.

As the accounting firm of PricewaterhouseCoopers explains in its analysis of the 2003 tax law, the rules are "quite favorable to taxpayers" because losses first reduce higher-rate gains. In other words, if you realized long-term gains on stock sales in February 2003 and again in November 2003, the first gain is in a "20-percent bucket" for the purpose of capital-gains tax while the second falls into the new 15-percent category. Any loss may be used to first offset the 20-percent gain, leaving less total tax to be paid.

Going forward, to determine how much tax you owe on your investments or how much loss you may use as an offset, add up short-term and long-term gains and losses. Include any capital-gains distributions made by mutual funds on transactions within the funds; they will be labeled on the 1099 information return you receive at year-end. Note, though, that some fund information returns may designate a "return of capital" that is not taxable but does reduce your cost basis.

**Tax tip:** In applying long-term losses against gains, don't forget gains on property other than securities. As attorney Julian Block points out, many taxpayers fail to realize that investment losses may be used to offset gains on the sale of vacation homes, collectibles, and rental property.

## STATE TAX ON GAINS

Most states with income taxes tax long-term capital gains and dividends at the same rates applied to earned income. Today, with most states facing declining revenues and budget deficits, even those states generally conforming to federal tax rules may be unlikely to reduce tax rates on capital gains and dividends.

# Keeping Costs Down

Don't overlook the expenses associated with investing. Some of these expenses may be deducted. Others may be minimized by selecting tax-managed and tax-exempt investment vehicles.

## Deductible Expenses

Many of the expenses associated with investing—including newsletter subscriptions, on-line services, money management fees, clerical help, and safe-deposit rental for the safe storage of stock certificates—are deductible as miscellaneous itemized expenses subject to the 2-percent floor on adjusted gross income. Like other miscellaneous itemized expenses, investment expenses are reported on Schedule A attached to Form 1040.

Some investment-related expenses—including the cost of attending stockholder meetings or investment seminars and any expenses associated with tax-exempt investments—are never deductible. Commissions are also not deductible, although they are added to the cost basis and reduce any taxable gain when you sell.

## Tax-efficient Mutual Funds

Many mutual funds are not particularly tax-efficient. Fund managers are typically compensated on pretax performance and therefore pay little attention to the tax consequences of their investment decisions. Actively managed funds, in particular, generate more capital gains because they have high turnover of securities within the portfolio.

However, there are two types of funds with lower turnover and lower capital-gains distributions. If you are investing in a taxable account (tax considerations are irrelevant in a tax-deferred retirement account), you may want to consider one or both of these fund categories for a portion of your investment portfolio.

- Index funds hold the same securities held by a specific stock market index; a popular example is the Standard & Poor's 500 index. There is no change within the fund portfolio unless the underlying index makes changes. Since this is a relatively rare occurrence, there are fewer transactions and therefore fewer capital-gains distributions to find their way to investors.
- Tax-managed funds, a relatively new breed, are specifically designed to hold turnover to a minimum. The managers of these funds are committed to weighing tax consequences before buying or selling securities within the portfolio. Gains within the portfolio may also be deliberately offset with sales to generate losses.

The Securities and Exchange Commission requires mutual funds to provide information about the tax efficiency of mutual fund investments. In addition to showing pretax returns, stock and bond mutual funds must include tables in their prospectuses showing after-tax returns for the past year, five years, and ten years. While the disclosure rules may help investors understand the impact of taxes on investment performance, they may not go far enough. The rules don't require funds to spell out their tax policies—or, indeed, to indicate whether portfolio managers pay any attention to tax considerations.

## Tax-exempt Bonds and Bond Funds

For high-bracket taxpayers living in high-tax states, tax-exempt municipal bonds—bought individually or through mutual funds—can be a way to minimize investment losses due to taxes. If you buy, stick to bonds issued by your own state for maximum tax efficiency. But don't be blinded by the lure of tax-free yields if you are not in a high bracket; as the table on page 175 shows, you'll probably come out ahead with taxable securities.

Municipal bonds are issued to pay for public projects. They may be *general obligation* bonds backed by the full faith and credit of the issuer, or *revenue* bonds backed by revenue from the particular project (such as a toll highway or bridge) funded by the bonds. General obligation bonds are a bit safer than revenue bonds.

Interest rates and bond prices move in opposite directions; bond prices rise when interest rates fall and decline when interest rates rise. So, although you are guaranteed to receive your full principal if you hold an individual bond to maturity, you may have to sell at a loss if you need your money early.

Bond mutual funds do not have maturity dates and shares can be sold at any time, although not necessarily at a profit. Bond funds also give you professional management along with built-in diversification to spread the risk. And bond funds provide a regular stream of income, either in cash or to reinvest.

Nonetheless, there can be advantages to buying individual bonds, especially if you:

- know that you will need the principal back at a specific date and not earlier. For example, parents may peg maturity dates to college tuition time.

- have enough money to diversify a bond portfolio. It may take at least $50,000 to purchase several different bond issues and thereby minimize the risk that one bond will lose value.

## COMPARING TAXABLE AND TAX-EXEMPT YIELDS

| | Tax-exempt Yields | | | | | |
|---|---|---|---|---|---|---|
| | 2% | 3% | 4% | 5% | 6% | 7% |
| Rates | Taxable Equivalents | | | | | |
| 10% | 2.22% | 3.33% | 4.44% | 5.56% | 6.67% | 7.78% |
| 15% | 2.35% | 3.53% | 4.71% | 5.88% | 7.06% | 8.24% |
| 25% | 2.67% | 4.00% | 5.33% | 6.67% | 8.00% | 9.33% |
| 28% | 2.78% | 4.17% | 5.56% | 6.94% | 8.33% | 9.72% |
| 33% | 2.99% | 4.48% | 5.97% | 7.46% | 8.96% | 10.45% |
| 35% | 3.08% | 4.62% | 6.15% | 7.69% | 9.23% | 10.77% |

## Investment Choices

While one or more tax-favored investment vehicles may fit into your long-range plans, don't make tax benefits your primary investment objective. First, be sure you've identified your personal goals and selected investments to help you attain those goals. Tax reduction is just one of many factors to consider. Other important considerations include your investment horizon and your attitude to risk.

Your *investment horizon* is the length of time before you will need your money. Short-term goals demand short-term investments. If you know you will face a college tuition bill in two years, don't invest in something such as individual stocks that you might be forced to sell at a loss. If you won't need to cash out until you retire in twenty years, on the other hand, you have time to ride market ups and downs in the interest of potentially greater returns.

Your *attitude toward risk* also plays a role in investment decisions. There are many types of risk—including the risk of losing purchasing power to inflation if you stick solely to "conservative" fixed-income investments—but you also want to be able to sleep at night.

Balance your investment horizon and your attitude toward risk in choosing your specific investments. For most people, once adequate cash reserves are in place, investments consist of a mix of stocks for growth and bonds for income. This can be accomplished by purchasing individual stocks and bonds or through buying shares of one or more mutual funds. For taxpayers in higher brackets, tax-deferred and tax-exempt investments can also play a role. If you are *not* in a high tax bracket, however, forget about tax-exempt bonds—at low tax rates, you will come out ahead with taxable investments. Whatever your choice of investment vehicles, good records are the key to tax savings.

## Record Keeping

Good investment records are essential if you are to reach your financial goals and keep taxes to a legal minimum. Without good records, you may find yourself paying tax on the same income twice.

But keeping good records does not mean keeping every piece of paper indefinitely. Doing so—in the face of a flood of trade confirmations, monthly and annual statements—will quickly overwhelm any filing system. Take heart. You can weed out investment records while retaining the documents necessary for long-term tax planning.

Refer to Chapter 1 for detailed suggestions about record keeping—and use the following Action Plan to streamline your efforts with respect to investment transactions.

## Action Plan

**Step One:** Keep year-end summary statements and 1099 forms from brokerage firms and mutual fund companies, but discard monthly and quarterly statements once you have received the year-end summaries.

**Step Two:** Use a notebook or ledger to record dividend and interest payments as they are received, paying special attention to reinvested dividends (see Step Three).

**Step Three:** Avoid double taxation on reinvested dividends by keeping detailed records on reinvestments, including the date, amount of the dividend, number of shares purchased, the per-share price, and any transaction fees.

**Step Four:** Keep ongoing records relating to deductible expenses associated with producing taxable income.

**Step Five:** Keep confirmations of purchases and sales—including the price, trade date, and any associated costs such as commissions—for at least four years following the year in which securities are sold. Records should be kept until 2008 for sales producing capital gains or losses in 2004.

## SEPTEMBER TAX TIPS

- **Third-quarter estimated tax payments** are due September 15.
- **Most dividends are now taxed** at a maximum rate of 15 percent; interest is still taxed at ordinary income rates topping out at 35 percent.
- **Investment income is taxed** in the year received, whether taken in cash or reinvested to purchase additional shares.
- **The capital-gains tax** on property held for more than twelve months before being sold is now at a maximum rate of 15 percent.
- **If you have kept accurate records,** you can reduce your tax bill when you sell partial holdings in a mutual fund by identifying the specific shares being sold.
- **Investment gains can be offset** by investment losses, with additional losses (up to $3,000 each year) used to reduce the tax on ordinary income.
- **Tax-efficient and tax-exempt investments** can reduce your total tax bill.
- **Good record keeping** is key to controlling investment-related taxes.

# Fourth Quarter: Tax Wrap-up

# CHAPTER 10

# October
## Audit Anguish

*Audit* is a word that strikes terror in taxpayers' souls—which is exactly what the IRS wants it to do. Don't be terrified. If you follow the advice throughout this book, and keep careful records, you can prove your case if questioned.

The Internal Revenue Service has three years to audit tax returns. That's three years from the date of filing, so that a federal income-tax return filed in April 2004 for the 2003 tax year is subject to audit until April 2007. That's the time frame for honest errors, for testing of possible gray areas in the tax code. If you "neglected" to report more than 25 percent of your income, the IRS has six years to audit your return. If you fail to file, or file a fraudulent return, there is no time limit. Taxpayers who play these games are fair game forever.

Relatively few federal tax returns have been audited in recent years, although the IRS has promised more audits with the additional money authorized in the 2003 federal budget. Those most likely to face audit are:

1. low-income taxpayers, because Congress and the IRS believe that the earned income credit is being misapplied
2. the self-employed, because small businesses tend to lack reliable accounting systems—and because the IRS suspects that cash income goes unreported

3. the wealthy, in a new campaign against abusive tax-avoidance schemes, including possible misuse of trusts and offshore accounts

Audit rates also vary from region to region. It may not seem fair, but where you live has a definite impact on how likely you are to be audited. A couple of years ago, when the national average of face-to-face audits for taxpayers with income of $100,000 or more was 0.47 percent, those living in Los Angeles were three times more likely to be audited, at a rate of 1.44 percent. Meanwhile, lucky high-income taxpayers in Georgia had the lowest audit rate, at 0.17 percent.

## AUDIT ODDS

| Individual Returns Filed | Percentage Audited |
|---|---|
| Total individual tax returns | 0.57% |
| $25,000–$50,000 in income | 0.23% |
| $50,000–$100,000 | 0.28% |
| $100,000 and over | 0.75% |
| Returns Filed by the Self-Employed | Percentage Audited |
| Under $25,000 in Schedule C income | 2.67% |
| $25,000–$100,000 in Schedule C income | 1.18% |
| $100,000 and over in Schedule C income | 1.45% |

Data for fiscal year 2002.

(Source: TRAC, Syracuse University)

# Shelters and Scams

It is altogether legal to avoid taxes. It is illegal to evade them. You legally shelter some income from taxation by contributing to an IRA or by taking a large mortgage on your house and deducting the interest payments. On the other hand, you move into evasion territory if you attempt to conceal income by placing it in an offshore bank account or create a phony loss on securities by artificially inflating the cost basis.

The line between avoidance and evasion blurs when efforts to avoid tax become what the IRS terms "abusive." While the IRS admits that "there is no hard and fast definition of abusive tax shelter arrangements," it also offers a description. On its Web site, www.irs.gov, the IRS notes that abusive tax schemes "involve transactions with little or no economic foundation." Instead they "exist solely to reduce taxes unrealistically," often by promising deductions larger than the amount invested. In these days of budget shortfalls, the states also aren't sitting idly by. For example, the California Franchise Tax Board launched a new round of audits in mid-2003, going after suspected tax cheats in abusive tax shelter cases.

Savvy taxpayers, like savvy investors, know that when something appears too good to be true, it generally is. But many taxpayers—far too many, the IRS believes—have been tempted to participate in abusive tax shelters in recent years by the prospect of big tax savings and an awareness that the IRS has had few resources available for audits. Many of these abusive shelters take the form of trusts. Trusts are often used in estate planning, and there are many legitimate trusts. But trusts established to hide the true ownership of assets and income are considered fraudulent. In fact, as the IRS points out, taxes must be paid on income or assets held in trust. If you control the assets in the trust, you owe the tax.

Many participants in abusive tax schemes are now getting

their comeuppance, facing criminal charges along with civil penalties. Evade tax by participating in abusive tax schemes and you are liable for taxes, interest, and penalties in addition to any criminal penalties that may be imposed. Civil penalties can be as much as 75 percent of the tax underpayment stemming from fraud. Criminal convictions may lead to fines of up to $250,000 and up to five years in prison.

For example, a promoter received a five-year prison term for creating and promoting sham trusts—and the five brothers who bought into his idea that they could use business trusts to conduct personal business and make personal purchases received prison sentences as well. In another case reported by the IRS Criminal Investigation Division, a Michigan dentist was sentenced to twenty-seven months in prison for failing to file federal income-tax returns and failing to report over $1.5 million in taxable income. To add embarrassment to his sentence, the judge also sentenced him to run a full-page newspaper ad explaining why he had been sentenced. Don't let this happen to you.

## AVOIDING ABUSIVE TRUSTS

The IRS warns of red flags identifying abusive trusts. Stay away from trust offerings that

- **promise to reduce** or eliminate income and self-employment taxes
- **suggest that personal expenses** paid by a trust are deductible
- **promise depreciation deductions** on your home and furnishings
- **use backdated** documents
- **charge high fees** to set up the trust, to be offset by promised tax benefits
- **use post office boxes** for trust addresses
- **uses terms** such as *pure trust, constitutional trust, sovereign trust,* or *unincorporated business trust*

Offshore trusts and credit cards are currently a major target of the IRS. The United States, unlike most other countries, requires citizens to pay tax on worldwide income. That means that offshore trusts and credit cards are illegal when they are used to hide income. In recent efforts to combat offshore arrangements, the IRS has obtained records of thousands of credit card accounts at offshore banks, obtained the identities of the cardholders, and tracked their spending patterns as a prelude to filing criminal and civil actions. In fighting tax shelters, the IRS is also going after the major accounting firms that have promoted these arrangements, fining the firms when they refuse to disclose the names of participating clients.

## Audit Roulette

You don't have to engage in a tax shelter or establish an abusive trust to have your return examined. All tax returns are screened for accuracy and all are subject to the IRS program matching W-2 and 1099 information returns against reported wages and other income. The IRS also uses a scoring process to identify returns worthy of examination. The process—and the "winning" scores—are kept secret, but tax professionals believe discrepancies are the key. One discrepancy that might bring your return to the attention of the IRS, for example, is claiming more deductions than seem to be reasonable for the amount of income you report. Another, perhaps less obvious, might be claiming a deduction for job-related moving expenses when you did not report the sale of your home in the prior location.

### Random Audits

In addition, because matching programs do not pick up many kinds of income, the IRS is expanding its program of random audits. The IRS has always conducted a certain number of random audits to test its own procedures. Under the dreaded Taxpayer Compliance Measurement Program (TCMP) of 1998, unlucky victims had to prove—and document—every single entry on their tax returns. That meant providing birth certificates and marriage certificates and backup for every piece of data. One reader of the *Wall Street Journal* likened the ordeal to "an autopsy without benefit of death."

The TCMP was suspended several years ago in the face of widespread displeasure with the intrusive nature of the investigations. This time around, in the newly minted National Research Program, the IRS promises not to be quite so intrusive. Nonetheless, almost fifty thousand taxpayer returns were to be subject to intense examination starting in 2003, with the goal of sharpening IRS understanding of tax cheating. Some seven thousand to eight thousand of this group remained ignorant of the scrutiny—their returns were examined in detail but they were not contacted. The rest were subject to various levels of examination, with an unlucky group of about two thousand coming close to the TCMP level of proof.

One tax monster that the IRS has promised not to reincarnate is the so-called "economic reality" or "lifestyle" audit, in which agents tried to determine if reported income could support a taxpayer's lifestyle. The goal was to look beyond the tax return itself to the entire life of the taxpayer. Under these audits, throwing a lavish wedding for your daughter or buying an expensive home could produce serious questioning by the IRS.

Lifestyle audits were considered so offensive that Congress put a halt to them in 1998, restricting them to situations where the IRS already has reason to believe that taxpayers are hiding income. Even then, taxpayers are to be given an opportunity to explain any apparent discrepancies. A lavish wedding might be partially funded by generous grandparents, for example, a fact that would not be immediately obvious to an IRS agent suspecting unreported income.

## NO SECRETS

Be forewarned: The various state taxing authorities conduct their own audits. In addition, the IRS exchanges information with state taxing agencies. If the outcome of an IRS audit affects your state income-tax liability, you should file an amended state return without waiting to be notified.

## Small Business Audits

If you report self-employment income, you may also fall into the IRS's Market Segment Specialization Program (MSSP). Aimed primarily at businesses, these audits rely on revenue agents trained to understand the particular "market segment." But individual taxpayers with Schedule C (self-employment) income can be vulnerable to MSSP audits as well. If you are an attorney, run a bed-and-breakfast, or own an automobile repair shop, there is an MSSP manual dealing with your business activities. In fact, if you run an escort service, there are IRS agents trained in the details of your business operations.

There are more than forty MSSP categories, including:

- architectural services
- art dealers
- attorneys
- auto body shops
- beauty salons and barbershops
- child care
- construction
- gas retailers
- grocery stores
- insurance agencies

- laundromats
- liquor stores
- real estate agents and brokers
- restaurants
- selling door-to-door
- travel agencies

The IRS claims that the MSSP program helps taxpayers by making agents knowledgeable about specific business operations and therefore saving taxpayer time. But what kinds of things does the IRS look at with its newly knowledgeable eyes? Well, if you run a bed-and-breakfast, you might want to be careful about deducting cable service for a single television set on the premises, because the IRS will know that you watch along with your guests. You might also want to think twice about deducting family vacations disguised as quests for antique furnishings for the B and B. In other words, the IRS has become sufficiently familiar with the business practices of enterprises in the MSSP fold to know where taxpayers try to shade legality by claiming fringe deductions.

## Red Flags

Want to stay under the IRS radar? Follow the Santa Claus rule: Make a list and check it twice. In other words, be extra careful in completing your federal income-tax return. For example, the IRS will be in touch if you forget to include your Social Security number on your tax return or make careless arithmetic errors. Watch out for transposed numbers, a simple error that can cause a lot of grief.

A single arithmetic mistake has lengthy ramifications, as numbers throughout your tax return build upon each other. You start with gross income, move to adjusted gross income, base itemized deductions on adjusted gross income—and a single error throws your entire tax return off-kilter. To minimize such mistakes, don't wait till the last minute to complete your return; haste generates errors. And try not to let yourself get too tired when working on your taxes. Many errors occur in the process of transferring numbers from a worksheet to the tax return. Using software, in fact, can eliminate many of these simple transcription errors—and filing electronically can eliminate mistakes generated by IRS clerks transferring data from paper returns.

You will most certainly hear from the IRS if there is a discrepancy between the income amounts you report and the amounts reported on W-2 forms from your employer or the 1099 information returns submitted by institutions paying interest, dividends, royalties, and other nonwage income. One couple got into trouble by taking what seemed like a simple shortcut. They reported consolidated interest and dividend income from several brokerage accounts held at the same firm—but the firm filed separate 1099 information returns for each individual account and their joint account. This isn't major trouble—but they did receive a "discrepancy notice" from the IRS and had to furnish an explanation.

There are other so-called red flags that may trigger unwanted attention from the IRS. For example, two taxpayers claiming the same dependent is a definite no-no. Working as a waiter or waitress and reporting little or no income in the form of tips is bound to draw attention.

## Action Plan

To simplify the process of tax preparation and reduce the errors that can lead to questions from the IRS:

**Step One:** Gather all tax-related documents—including W-2 and 1099 forms—before you begin; match your own income records against all the information returns you've received.

## Action Plan

**Step Two:** Enter tax data on a worksheet or in tax preparation software, then check all the information for accuracy before entering it on the tax return or turning it over to a tax preparer.

**Step Three:** Make sure you keep good records to substantiate your return, especially in areas—such as home office or casualty deductions—that may be challenged by the IRS.

**Step Four:** When you finish preparing your tax return or receive your completed return from a tax practitioner, review it carefully to be sure nothing is omitted and that no numbers are transposed or entered incorrectly.

### Legitimate Claims

Other claims, while they may initially raise suspicions at the IRS, can be justified. You should never hesitate to reduce your taxes by any legitimate means, so long as you have the appropriate documentation to back your claim.

As an example, many taxpayers refuse to claim home office deductions for fear doing so will trigger an audit. Yet claiming expenses associated with a home office is absolutely legitimate for a home-based business using a space exclusively for business. In fact, recent regulations issued by the IRS have clarified the home office deduction and made it available to more taxpayers. (See Chapter 7 for more details.) Even a claim for unusually high medical expenses or charitable contributions will be accepted with proper documentation. In these cases, in fact, many tax professionals believe that it's wise to enclose a brief letter of explanation with your income-tax return.

Assuming that you are not involved in tax evasion, the best

way to prevent an audit is to be scrupulous in retaining backup documents for the information on your tax return. Keep good records along with the receipts to document those records—you don't want to rely on memory to reconstruct records two or three years after the fact—and make sure that your return is accurately prepared.

---

### FUG-GED-ABOUT-IT

Some expenses simply cannot be deducted. The IRS will automatically disallow claims for:

- **losses on the sale** of your home
- **medical deductions** for health club dues or diet foods
- **itemized deductions** for sales tax or car registration
- **personal interest,** other than on a qualified home mortgage
- **personal insurance,** other than long-term-care insurance
- **excessive** job-related moving expenses

---

## Audit Notice

*Audit* is a fearful word. But there are actually several levels of IRS scrutiny. Some are far easier to deal with than others.

### Discrepancies

The first level is not really an audit. It takes the form of a computer-generated "notice of adjustment," typically noting an arithmetic error in your return or pointing out a discrepancy between your return and a 1099 filed by an institution reporting income such as interest or dividends. Attorney Frederick W. Daily, author of *Stand Up to the IRS*, notes that you shouldn't automatically pay up, as these notices are often wrong. In fact, it happened to him one year when he mistakenly reported money market fund returns as interest instead of dividends—the IRS computer didn't see the earnings on the appropriate line of the return and spit out a deficiency notice, billing for tax, interest, and penalties.

If you suspect a notice is wrong, contest it by calling the IRS and then sending a letter explaining your position. Be patient, because the IRS is notoriously slow to respond. If you continue to receive notices until the matter is resolved, as is likely, send a photocopy of your original letter in response to each notice.

## The Real Thing

There are three levels of actual audit: correspondence, office, and field. Most audits of individual returns fall into the first two categories.

A *correspondence audit* consists of a written notice from the IRS, typically asking for documentation for one or more entries on your income-tax return. In these targeted audits, the IRS is most likely to question itemized deductions, dependency exemptions, and—a particular favorite—casualty and theft losses. Send the documentation to back your claim—copies, please, not the originals—and that should resolve the matter.

Going face-to-face with an IRS agent in an *office audit* is another matter—although it may be reassuring to know that at least one in ten office audits results in no change. A handful even lead to money being refunded to the taxpayer.

In an office audit, you are asked to appear at an IRS office to discuss specific questions relating to the return you filed for a given year. Bring only records backing up your position on the issue or issues in question—you don't want to open up new areas for questioning—and have those records organized by topic so you don't waste time fumbling for documents during the interview. If the agent asks for information about a topic not previously scheduled for discussion, or brings up reporting for another year, politely say that you don't see the relevance to the matter under discussion.

The IRS prefers face-to-face audits because, while they are more labor-intensive for a chronically strapped agency, they are also far more lucrative. In 2000, face-to-face audits returned an average of $9,500 apiece against $1,500 brought in from document matching.

But taxpayers do have rights. You may ask that the meeting be rescheduled if the original date is not convenient. You may stop the audit if it ventures into fields that were not raised in advance; simply say that you need more time to prepare and to gather the necessary documentation, and a follow-up meeting will be scheduled.

*Field audits,* where the IRS comes to your home or place of business, are typically reserved for returns filed by businesses, although they sometimes target individuals with complicated financial affairs. These audits are wide-open, and the IRS can delve into all details of your finances.

## Go It Alone?

You may bring your tax preparer along or send your tax preparer in your place, if he or she is approved to appear before the IRS. Approved representatives include CPAs, enrolled agents, and tax attorneys.

Many professionals believe that it's generally a good idea to send a representative in your place. Professionals know how to negotiate an agreement. They know how to deal with the IRS. Nervous individual taxpayers may talk too much and wind up raising new questions from the IRS agent. If you decide to go it alone and feel that you must make small talk, stick to the weather—and don't bring up your vacation trip to a warm climate to escape the cold. If you do, the examiner may wonder where you got the money to make the trip. The last thing you want to do is raise any new subjects for discussion.

On the other hand, if you've been informed that only one fairly clear-cut area is under consideration and you're pretty sure you can prove your case, you may want to calculate the cost in terms of a trade-off. If the end result is likely to be less than $1,000 in additional tax, interest, and penalties, it may not be worthwhile to pay a CPA's hourly rate to spend several hours preparing for an audit and then a couple of hours attending the audit. At best, it may be a wash in terms of dollars and cents, although you may prefer not to face an auditor's grilling in person.

## State Audits

By and large, the states are content to let the IRS investigate income-tax filings, reserving most of their direct attention for gift and estate-tax returns. But (in addition to the tax shelter investigations begun by some states) many high-tax states routinely—and aggressively—pursue people who have homes in two states but claim residency in the state with little or no income tax. Florida has no state income tax—and New York State is particularly active in going after snowbirds, the folks who live in Florida in the winter months and move back north in the summer.

Technically speaking, these folks are Florida residents for income tax purposes so long as they spend at least 183 days a year in Florida. But it takes a bit more to prove the point to New York State. One snowbird of my acquaintance had to give up a precious New York apartment to make the case that he was in fact a Florida resident. You may not have a rent-controlled apartment to relinquish—but it's a good idea to shift voter registration, driver's license, club memberships, and religious affiliations to the state where you want to claim residency. It may also be wise to draft a new will and, if you hold on to a residence in a Northern state, move valued possessions to the Southern locale.

The states, like the federal government, can tax the worldwide income of residents. Nonresidents, by contrast, owe tax only on income acquired within the state. There's a big difference—and, despite offsetting tax credits, you may wind up owing a much larger tax bill if you can't prove that you reside in only one state.

New York is just one example. High-tax California has a similar relationship with no-tax Nevada. Dividing your time between any two states, especially where one has much higher state income taxes than the other, can lead to questions from tax authorities—questions best answered by establishing and documenting a single state of residence. That documentation can include a diary showing day-to-day activities, along with telephone bills and credit card statements showing your whereabouts.

## After the Audit

Most office audits involving federal income tax end with an on-the-spot agreement. You will walk away with no change in the return under examination, be in the lucky position of being owed a refund, or—more likely—owe additional tax. If you are entitled to a refund, the IRS will pay interest. If you owe more tax, you will have to pay interest. Guess which interest rate is higher? The IRS, as always, comes out ahead.

If you owe substantial amounts of additional tax, and can't pay all at once, you may be able to reach an agreement to pay in installments. If your outstanding tax liability is $25,000 or less, you may request an installment agreement by filing Form 9465. You must agree to pay the outstanding amount within five years. There is a user fee plus late payment penalties and interest on the unpaid balance. See Chapter 3 for more on installment agreements.

Or, if you disagree with the auditor's findings, you may appeal the decision. While appeals often result in a reduction of the additional tax (plus interest and penalties) assessed in an audit, appeals can take a long time. This can be good, if you look at it as giving you time to come up with cash to pay the tax bill. It's not so good from the standpoint that, during the appeals process, interest continues to mount on your unpaid tax bill—unless you pay the tax in anticipation of filing for a refund if your appeal is successful.

## "FRIVOLOUS" APPEALS

While every taxpayer is entitled to appeal an IRS determination, the agency frowns on "frivolous" appeals that consume time and resources. Such positions contend that the income tax is not valid, that it is voluntary and therefore need not be paid, that the person or type of income is not subject to the tax—all arguments that the tax court has rejected as baseless. File such an appeal in an attempt to stall tax payments and you may face a penalty of up to $25,000.

The first step in an appeal—and the last, for most people—is typically an administrative review within the IRS. You may request an appeals conference, an informal meeting in person or by telephone to review the issues in dispute. You may act for yourself or designate a representative—such as a CPA or an enrolled agent—who is certified to appear before the IRS. The toll-free number to contact the IRS Appeals office is 1-877-457-5055. When you call, ask about "fast-track mediation," a service that is being offered by the IRS as a speedier alternative to the typically lengthy appeals process.

Whether you represent yourself at an in-person appeals conference, or send a professional representative in your place, be prepared. Frederick Daily suggests organizing your documents by creating a file folder or three-ring binder and grouping documents by topic. Provide the auditor with a duplicate folder or binder with copies of all the documents so that he or she can follow along as you make your presentation. A written summary and/or adding machine tape for each category can be helpful. And, where appropriate, you may want to employ pictorial evidence—a good example might be a photo of your professional-looking home office to bolster your claim of a home office deduction.

As a last resort, if the stakes are high, you may take your case to court. The U.S. Tax Court, for cases where no more than $50,000 is at stake, has a distinct advantage: You do not have to pay the amount in dispute before the case is heard. By contrast, the District Court and the U.S. Court of Federal Claims hear tax cases only after you have paid the tax and requested a refund. But court cases are expensive, the IRS generally (although not always) is the victor, and you may want to think twice about whether a court appeal is worthwhile. In any case, this is definitely the time to seek professional advice.

In the end, if you are unable to pay the full amount, even in installments, you may seek an "offer in compromise." If there is a genuine dispute about the tax that is due, if you simply can't pay the tax and still meet basic living expenses, or if there are exceptional circumstances making efforts at collection unfair, the IRS may agree to accept smaller amounts over a period of time. However, you may not apply for a compromise if you have filed for bankruptcy or if you have failed to file past tax returns. Once you are accepted into the program—and have paid the $150 application fee levied as of November 1, 2003—you will give up any tax refunds for prior years, the current year, and very possibly for future years as well.

Taxpayers accepted into the program after appeals are exhausted wind up paying far less than they owe. But don't count on this solution to your tax problems—only a small number of the taxpayers applying for this program are accepted, often after long delays. The entire offer-in-compromise program, according to a 2003 report by the IRS Oversight Board, is in need of an overhaul and may be facing drastic change.

## Action Plan

**Step One:** Request an appeals conference, in person or by telephone, to review disputed audit results; ask about "fast-track mediation" to speed the process.

**Step Two:** If your dispute involves no more than $50,000 and you are still unhappy after the appeals conference, take your appeal to the U.S. Tax Court; you do not have to pay the disputed amount until the case is resolved.

**Step Three:** For larger amounts, consider taking your case to the District Court or the U.S. Court of Federal Claims; taking this tack means paying the disputed amount and hoping for a refund.

**Step Four:** If all appeals fail and the disputed amount is less than $25,000, try to arrange an installment agreement to spread out payments over five years.

**Step Five:** In desperate situations—where you truly cannot pay the tax—request an "offer in compromise" to reduce the tax you must pay.

## TAX TIPS FOR OCTOBER

- **Most audits are conducted within three years** of the filing date for the tax return in question.
- **The IRS looks for discrepancies** on tax returns—and for illegal and abusive tax "shelters."
- **The IRS periodically conducts random audits** to generate information.
- **Audits can be conducted** by correspondence, in an IRS field office, or—for businesses and individuals with complicated affairs—at the taxpayer's office.
- **Taxpayers may send a designated representative** to an audit in their place.
- **You may appeal** the result of an audit if you feel it is unjustified.

# CHAPTER 11

# November
## Life Happens

Getting a handle on your taxes is one thing. Getting a handle on your life is another. You can master your taxes, then find that changing circumstances require a new approach. Julie gets married. Jason gets divorced. Brittany is supporting her aging parents, while Martin copes with the uninsured costs of his own ill health. Whenever your life changes in ways that affect your finances and, as a result, your tax return, taking action promptly—instead of procrastinating—can help you save money and stay ahead of the game.

## Tying the Knot

Whether it's you or your adult children planning a wedding, take your eye off the gold ring—at least temporarily—to focus on related tax planning.

First, think about the wedding date with an eye to tax savings. For many couples, getting married in late December will produce a more favorable tax picture than getting married in early January. That's because your new spouse will be entitled to an exemption for the entire year. On returns filed in 2004 for the 2003 tax year, each exemption is worth $3,050.

For couples with comparable his-and-hers incomes, on the other hand, the "marriage penalty" may make it worth waiting until January to tie the knot.

## The Marriage Penalty

The marriage penalty is much talked about and little understood. It is not an actual penalty written into the tax code to deter people from getting married. Instead, it is a historical accident stemming from our graduated income-tax system and our policy of viewing married couples as a single taxpaying unit. Other developed nations, tax professor Edward J. McCaffery points out in his illuminating book *Taxing Women*, use a system of separate filing under which husbands and wives are treated as individuals. With separate filing, each spouse fills out an individual tax return and pays tax under an individual rate schedule. As a result, neither is pushed into a higher tax bracket by combining earnings with a spouse.

The primary culprit under the graduated U.S. tax system, according to Larchmont, New York, tax attorney Julian Block, is "bracket creep—higher income means a higher tax rate." As two singles, most of each income may fit into a lower tax bracket; once married, income is combined and pushes the couple into a higher tax bracket. In other words, two separate incomes might each be taxed at 15 percent—when added together, part or all of the second income is pushed into the 25-percent bracket. For example: Using nice round numbers, Ned and Nina each earn $100,000. Filing separately, each is in the 28-percent tax bracket. As married filing jointly, their combined income of $200,000 puts them in the 33-percent tax bracket.

The other element pushing married couples into the penalty box is that the standard deduction for married couples filing jointly has long been less than twice that for two single taxpayers. For the 2002 tax year, when the standard deduction was

$4,700 for singles ($9,400 for two single taxpayers) and $7,850 for married couples filing jointly, the marriage "penalty" was $1,550 ($9,400 – $7,850 = $1,550).

Marriage penalty relief has arrived, at least in part, with the big tax changes of 2003. There are two dramatic changes:

1. The standard deduction for married taxpayers is now twice that for single taxpayers—at least for two years. If Congress takes no action, 2005 will see a reversion to the pre-2003 arrangement. Meanwhile, for the 2003 tax year, the standard deduction for singles increases to $4,750 ($4,850 for 2004), while the standard deduction for married taxpayers filing jointly jumps from $7,850 to $9,500 ($9,700 for 2004).

2. The 15-percent tax bracket for joint filers has expanded to twice the size of the bracket for a single taxpayer. The expansion was to begin in 2005 and become fully effective in 2008, but under the 2003 law it became effective immediately. Other brackets remain the same, however, so couples with joint income pushing them above the 15-percent bracket will continue to suffer a marriage penalty.

In fact, marriage penalties and bonuses are interwoven throughout some sixty provisions of the Internal Revenue Code. Mark Luscombe, federal tax analyst for tax publishers CCH, points to another little-recognized penalty in the capital-gains tax. A married couple can deduct only $3,000 in capital losses on a joint return, an amount that (despite much discussion) hasn't changed under the new law. Two single taxpayers can deduct $3,000 apiece. On the other hand, it may be small comfort, but one spouse can offset gains in the stock market with losses sustained by the other.

## TAX FILING FOR THE NEWLY WIDOWED

If your spouse died at any time during the year, you are considered married for the entire year and may file your return as married filing jointly. For subsequent years, unless you remarry, you will file as a single taxpayer. But there is an exception. If you have dependent children and have not remarried, you may file for two years after the year of your partner's death as a "qualifying widow(er) with dependent child." This is a special category that lets you use joint return tax rates and the highest standard deduction amount for two years until you must file (unless you remarry) as single or as head of household.

# Parting of the Ways

Your filing status is determined by your marital status on the last day of the year. If you get married in December, you can file jointly for the year. If your divorce becomes final in December, you may file as a single taxpayer for the entire year.

Filing status is the easy part. Divorce presents a whole other array of tax complications, with issues arising from the custody of children and the division of assets.

## The Children of Divorce

The parent who has custody for most of the year is the parent who is allowed to claim a tax exemption for the child. This is true even if the noncustodial parent provides more than half of the child's financial support. However, you can change this arrangement with a written agreement giving custody to one parent and the tax exemption to the other.

The parent in the higher tax bracket generally benefits most from claiming the dependency exemption—unless that parent has such high income that exemptions are phased out. For the 2003 tax year, exemptions begin to phase out when adjusted gross income exceeds $139,500 for single taxpayers, $209,250 for married couples filing jointly. Exemptions disappear entirely when AGI exceeds $262,000 for single taxpayers and $331,750 for married couples filing jointly. In addition, taxpayers subject to the alternative minimum tax (see Chapter 12) may not claim any dependency exemptions. If Georgette earns $180,000 a year and must pay the alternative minimum tax, while George earns $80,000 and can forget about the AMT, George will benefit from the dependency exemption even if Georgette has primary custody. If their divorce is amicable—at least as far as the children are concerned—they can sign an agreement giving him the exemption.

## Action Plan

**Step One:** If you have agreed that one of you will have custody of the children while the other claims the exemption, the custodial parent should complete Form 8332 releasing the exemption to the noncustodial parent, and attach the form to the income-tax return. The exemption can be released permanently or one year at a time. The latter is generally a wise move because it gives you flexibility to adapt to changing circumstances by renegotiating your agreement.

**Step Two:** Be careful in structuring alimony and child-support payments. If you will make payments to your ex-spouse, you may prefer that they be alimony because alimony is deductible—even though your ex will owe tax on the income. Your ex-spouse may prefer child support because the

## Action Plan

payments are neutral, neither deductible nor taxable. The IRS prefers accuracy—and does not like child-support payments (or property settlements) masquerading as alimony. The penalty, if caught, is paying the taxes that should have been paid plus interest, and penalties.

### Alimony

Because alimony is deductible, Uncle Sam absorbs a large part of the cost—fully 35 percent of the amount paid in alimony by high-bracket taxpayers. This deduction tempts some folks to cloak child-support payments in the guise of alimony. Don't do it. At the very least, get expert legal advice. If this "alimony" ends within six months of a specified event, such as a child turning 18 or graduating from high school, Norristown, Pennsylvania, attorney Lynne Gold-Bikin warns, the IRS will assume it was child support all along and impose penalties.

Because alimony is deductible, in fact, the IRS imposes fairly stringent requirements. In order to qualify, the payments must be in cash, check, or money order, you may not be living in the same house, and the payments must be made under a written divorce or separation agreement. In addition, the obligation to make payments must end at the death of the recipient.

And there's one more requirement. The IRS does not like property settlements disguised as alimony and pays particular attention to these two scenarios:

1. alimony payments in the first postdivorce year exceeding the average of the payments in the following two years by $15,000 or more

2. alimony payments in the second year exceeding payments in the third year by $15,000 or more

If either of these events occurs, then the IRS will "recapture" a portion of the alimony deducted in the first two years by adding it back to the payer's taxable income in the third year. There are exceptions to the recapture rule, but this is a particularly complicated portion of the Internal Revenue Code. Be sure you get good legal and tax advice.

As the payer, you may deduct alimony payments whether you use the standard deduction or itemize. But you must file Form 1040 and not either of the short forms, 1040EZ or 1040A. As the recipient, you must also use Form 1040 to report the alimony you receive.

**Tax tip:** Alimony is considered compensation for the purpose of making contributions to an Individual Retirement Account. If you have no other earned income but receive alimony, you may contribute to an IRA to build future retirement income.

## THE STATES OF DIVORCE

Most states divide the property of divorcing couples according to principles of "equitable distribution." But "equitable" is not necessarily "equal." The partner who contributed more to the marriage often walks away with more.

Nine states (Arizona, California, Idaho, Louisiana, Nevada, New Mexico, Texas, Washington, and Wisconsin) are "community property" states. In these states, with some variation, money earned during the marriage and property acquired during the marriage is divided equally in divorce. Exceptions are property purchased with separate funds as well as property given to or inherited by one spouse and kept separate by that spouse. If property cannot be identified as separate property, it will generally be deemed community property.

## Dividing Property in Divorce

For most people, the house and the pension are the two biggest assets to be split. But everything is up for grabs in a divorce—including bank accounts and securities along with stock options and business property. Some of these assets can be hard to value and therefore hard to divide.

When assets are transferred from one spouse to the other, whether during marriage or as part of divorce proceedings, the transfer is not a taxable event. Transfers are considered "incident to divorce" if they are related to the end of the marriage and if they take place no more than one year later.

But taxes do come into play when divvied-up assets are later sold. The tax is based on the difference between the selling price and the original cost basis. The cost basis is the purchase price (plus acquisition costs such as commissions) that, when subtracted from the sales price, determine profit or loss. A transfer from one spouse to the other does not change the cost basis of the asset. If John transfers securities to Jane as part of the property settlement, the securities were purchased for $20,000 and have a market value of $100,000 at the time of the divorce, Jane will owe capital-gains tax on the entire $80,000 in profit if she sells right after the divorce. If she holds the securities for several years and sells the shares for $200,000, she will owe capital-gains tax on $180,000. Of course, if the value drops back to $20,000 by the time of sale, there would be no profit and therefore no tax.

As you place a value on all your tangible assets, be sure to consider their after-tax value—especially if you plan to sell and will face capital-gains tax on appreciation. As New York attorney Eleanor Brietel Alter notes, equal market value does not necessarily mean equal after-tax value. Transferring a house is temporarily tax-neutral but could leave the recipient with a tax bill when the house is sold. Withdrawing $100,000 from an IRA produces an immediate tax penalty, while withdrawing the same amount from a checking account has no tax consequences.

## Retirement Benefits

The money you've put aside for retirement in most tax-deferred plans is so thoroughly protected by federal law that it can't be thrown into the pot of assets to be divided in divorce without a special document called a qualified domestic relations order or QDRO (familiarly pronounced "quadro"). Without a QDRO, a transfer of retirement assets may disqualify the plan and make its assets immediately taxable.

With a defined contribution plan such as a 401(k), where there are actual dollars in the employee's account available to divide, the QDRO will create a separate account in the second spouse's name. That spouse can roll his or her portion into an IRA or, if the employer's plan permits, leave the money in place and make investment decisions within the plan.

With a defined-benefit pension, where monthly pension benefits will eventually be paid under a formula set by the employer, the QDRO may divide the anticipated amount at the date of the divorce. The partner who earned the pension may receive a larger benefit based on future earnings, while the other partner may receive a pension based on the value at the date of divorce plus projected future investment earnings on that amount.

Individual Retirement Accounts are the only tax-favored retirement vehicles that are not "qualified" plans. IRAs may therefore be divided without a QDRO, pursuant to the terms of the divorce decree. The entire IRA may be shifted to an ex-spouse by changing the name on the account. Or an IRA may be divided by rolling over the agreed-upon amount (all or part of the account balance) or by making a direct trustee-to-trustee transfer.

## Action Plan

**Step One:** In dividing assets in divorce, try to make assets comparable in terms of the original cost basis, the current value, and the after-tax value.

**Step Two:** In dividing a stock portfolio, you may want to tell the broker to divide it so that each has the designated proportion of the whole. If batches of specific securities were bought at different times, each batch should be divided into two groups with the same cost basis and after-tax value, thereby avoiding a situation where one partner gets appreciated stocks and the other partner receives stocks that have lost value.

**Step Three:** In considering whether to keep the family home—a major asset for most couples—pay particular attention to the tax consequences. Under current law, assuming that a house has been owned and occupied as a principal residence for two of the last five years, a single taxpayer may keep as much as $250,000 of profit on the sale of a home without owing tax. A married couple may exclude up to $500,000 of profit. In a relatively new wrinkle, if one spouse moves out pursuant to a separation agreement or divorce decree, that spouse is still considered an owner for the purpose of the exclusion. (For more on home sales, see Chapter 7.)

**Step Four:** Because pension benefits cannot be transferred to another person, even as part of a divorce settlement, without a qualified domestic relations order, start the QDRO wheels in motion early in divorce negotiations. Plan administrators may not actually divide the benefits until the divorce is final, but, without a QDRO, a transfer of retirement assets may disqualify the plan and lose its tax-favored status. If you have multiple retirement plans from jobs at different companies, you must obtain a separate QDRO for each plan.

## "Innocent" Spouses

Once a joint tax return has been signed, the law assumes that either party can be held responsible for the entire tax that is due. The result: A marriage may be over but tax penalties linger on. As Mark Luscombe of CCH has commented, "You might call this the ultimate marriage penalty—being stuck with the bad tax bills of a former spouse."

But it is now possible to apply for three distinct types of relief from the tax tangles of a former marriage:

- Innocent spouse relief can be sought when a spouse did not know, and had no reason to know, of misstatements on a joint return. This claim, because it is so broad, is tough to justify to the satisfaction of the IRS.
- Separating liabilities does not demand total innocence before relief can be granted and is therefore easier to obtain. The IRS must show that you had "actual knowledge" of a spouse's understatement of income in order to deny your claim.
- Equitable relief may work for people not eligible for either of the first two forms of relief. It may also provide a shield when the issue is underpayment, not just understatement of tax. In an example provided by Mr. Luscombe: Your joint return showed an accurate tax liability of $2,000. Instead of paying the bill, your spouse left town. Based on who earned what, you may qualify for equitable relief instead of being stuck with the bill.

To request either innocent spouse relief or allocation of liabilities, file Form 8857. For more information, see IRS Publications #971, "Innocent Spouse Relief (and Separation of Liability and Equitable Relief)" and #504, "Divorced or Separated Individuals."

## Action Plan

In addition to the major tax issues in divorce, pay attention to these housekeeping details:

**Step One:** Adjust your Form W-4 to accurately reflect withholding allowances in your new situation.

**Step Two:** Adjust quarterly estimated-tax payments to reflect alimony payments you will receive during the year.

**Step Three:** Request detailed bills for legal services connected with your divorce. The cost of obtaining the divorce is not deductible, but costs associated with tax advice or specifically associated with obtaining alimony are deductible.

**Step Four:** Review—and change, if necessary—beneficiary designations on IRAs and life insurance. These assets bypass your will and go directly to the named beneficiary. Fail to change that beneficiary and your ex may get a windfall.

## Helping Aging Parents

If your life includes providing financial support for aging parents, there are a number of tax breaks that can help to ease the burden.

In general, a dependency exemption may be claimed only if you provide more than half of the person's total support during the calendar year—*and* if that person earns no more than the amount of the dependency exemption ($3,050 for the 2003 tax year). But there are two exceptions to this rule:

1. **Multiple support.** Suppose you, your brothers, and your sisters all contribute to your mother's support. No one of you provides more than half of her support. Nonetheless,

one of you (whichever one you all agree on) may claim the dependency exemption so long as all of you together supply over half of her support and one of you provides more than 10 percent. To claim the exemption, each sibling contributing more than 10 percent must sign a Multiple Support Declaration (IRS Form 2120). All of the forms should be filed with the tax return of the person claiming the exemption. This is a one-year agreement, so you can take turns claiming the exemption if you wish to do so.

2. **Definition of income.** The income limitation refers only to income that is subject to tax. Social Security retirement benefits and municipal bond interest are generally not taxable. So, if your mother receives $5,000 a year in Social Security retirement benefits, $2,000 in dividends from a municipal bond fund, and $3,000 in taxable income, you can still claim her as a dependent and take the exemption. Of course, to do so, you must provide more than half of her support or enter into a Multiple Support Agreement.

If your parents live with you and you pay for a caregiver so that you can go to work, the cost is not deductible but you may be entitled to an offsetting tax credit. This is the same credit available for child care; it is income-based and the maximum is $2,400 for one qualifying individual, $4,800 for two.

In filing their own federal income-tax returns, people age 65 and over (or those permanently and totally disabled) may be entitled to both a tax credit and a higher standard deduction. The tax credit is subject to severe income restrictions; either adjusted gross income cannot exceed $25,000 or nontaxable income must be less than $7,500 for a married couple if both spouses are eligible. The increased standard deduction is available to any taxpayer age 65 and over (or blind). For the 2003 tax year, the standard deduction is increased by $950 per person for each of a married couple filing jointly who is age 65 or over (or blind); it is increased by $1,150 for single taxpayers.

# Medical Expenses

Ill health and measures taken to maintain good health may also yield some tax breaks, although there's a major stumbling block in the way of actually claiming deductions for medical expenses—you may do so only for costs exceeding 7.5 percent of adjustable gross income. For most people, especially if they have health insurance picking up some of the costs, this requirement rules out a deduction. According to the IRS, more than one-third of taxpayers itemize deductions, but fewer than 6 percent claim medical expenses.

## Medical Deductions

However, many people do not have health insurance and may be able to claim a deduction. Many with health insurance do not have dental insurance, so root canals and crowns may produce a deduction. It's worth tracking expenses and keeping receipts just in case a deduction proves possible. In fact, if you provide support for an elderly parent and pay his or her medical expenses, you may be able to claim those expenses along with your own. For example: Brittany widens doorways in her home and puts in a ramp to accommodate her father's wheelchair; the cost is a deductible medical expense. A few years later, when her father moves to an assisted-living facility, the medical cost component of the monthly fee is deductible. Still later, if a nursing home is necessary because Dad needs round-the-clock medical care, the entire cost will be deductible.

If you do qualify for a medical expense deduction, be sure to include all the deductible items. Some—such as doctor visits and surgery—are obvious. Others may not be. Here are some examples of items deductible as medical expenses (for a complete list, see IRS Publication #502):

- acupuncture treatments
- an air conditioner necessary to relieve symptoms of allergies
- exercise programs recommended by a doctor to treat a specific condition
- extra rent or utilities needed to provide space for a nurse or attendant
- home improvements such as ramps to accommodate a wheelchair, railings, support bars, and other structural changes to help someone with a physical handicap
- programs to end smoking or combat alcoholism
- telephone enhancements for the hearing impaired
- transportation costs to obtain medical care, at 13 cents per mile (in 2003) plus parking and tolls
- lodging while away from home for medical treatment
- weight-loss programs as treatment for disease—and, in a new ruling, the IRS will recognize obesity (diagnosed by a physician) as a disease

With the exception of insulin, only prescription drugs are deductible. However, nonprescription items such as bandages, thermometers, crutches, and blood-sugar test kits are deductible.

Cosmetic surgery is deductible only if it is related to an injury or illness or is needed to correct a deformity. Merely improving appearance does not qualify. Thus the IRS has specifically ruled that breast reconstruction after a mastectomy and vision correction by laser surgery are deductible expenses. Tooth whitening to correct discoloration is not.

Health insurance premiums are deductible to the extent that, combined with other medical expenses, they exceed 7.5 percent of AGI. However, health insurance premiums paid by self-employed individuals are now fully tax-deductible (see Chapter 5).

Premiums paid for long-term care policies meeting federal regulations are also deductible, subject to specific dollar limits at various ages (see table). Benefits paid under these policies are also largely tax-free. They are entirely tax-free if the contract pays only actual expenses or a set dollar amount per day for a terminally ill patient. They are tax-free up to $210 per day under a per-diem contract for a chronically ill patient.

---

## MAXIMUM DEDUCTIBLE LONG-TERM-CARE PREMIUMS FOR 2003

| Age | Amount |
|---|---|
| 40 or less | $250 |
| 41–50 | $470 |
| 51–60 | $940 |
| 61–70 | $2,510 |
| 71 and over | $3,130 |

---

## TAX TIPS FOR NOVEMBER

- **Choose your wedding date** with an eye to tax consequences; getting married in December can give you an extra exemption for the year or subject you sooner to the marriage "penalty."
- **The tax implications of divorce** revolve around alimony, child support, and the division of property.
- **There are tax breaks** that can ease the financial burdens associated with caring for aging parents.
- **Medical expenses are deductible** to the extent that they exceed 7.5 percent of adjusted gross income.

## CHAPTER 12

# December
## Pulling It All Together

As the days dwindle down to a precious few, there are still some things you can do to save money in the months and years ahead. In fact, while tax planning should be a year-round affair, December is a critical month. It might be called the procrastinator's golden opportunity. With very few exceptions—for example, you have until the date you file your tax return next spring to make an IRA contribution for this year—December presents your last chance to reduce taxes for the current calendar year.

In addition to the tax-reduction measures that you can still take in December for the current year, you can use this year's tax data to manage your tax liability in the years ahead. Plan now, instead of procrastinating, and you should be able to make a serious dent in future tax bills.

## Investment Moves

As you near the end of the year and the final reckoning on this year's income tax, you may want to consider making some changes in your investment portfolio. You may want to move toward investments yielding greater tax benefits (see Chapter 9 for ideas on tax-efficient investments)—or unload some losing investments. Selling losers is one of the biggest year-end tax-saving possibilities.

## Taking Losses

Following the stock market turmoil of the last few years, many investors have paper losses on investments—their investments are worth much less now than they were when purchased, but the losses are only on paper, not translated into dollars and cents until the securities are sold. If you're in this boat, you may want to sell the losers before year-end to secure the tax benefits. As discussed in Chapter 9, losses can offset capital gains to reduce your tax liability. If you have more losses than gains, up to $3,000 of the excess amount may be applied to offset ordinary income; any amount beyond $3,000 can be carried forward to future tax years.

If you sell any property subject to capital-gains tax—including securities, real estate, and collectibles—you must file Schedule D, "Capital Gains and Losses," with Form 1040. You may not use either of the short tax forms, 1040EZ or 1040A.

## Doing the Wash

Perhaps you hold some securities that have lost considerable value, but you think they are solid investments and expect them to revive. You could sell them before year-end and use the loss to offset gains on other investments. However, if you intend to then buy the same securities at the current lowered price and hold them going forward, be careful.

The IRS forbids losses on "wash sales" of this nature—unless there are at least thirty days between the sale and the purchase. The way around the wash-sale rule is to sell the loser and buy something that is similar but not identical. In general this means buying the stock of another company in the same industry or shares of a mutual fund with similar but not identical objectives. Your financial adviser can help you make an appropriate selection.

Avoiding wash-sale restrictions is easier with bonds than with stocks. Replacement bonds are typically not considered "substantially identical" and therefore do not fail the wash-sale test if they are issued by a different agency, have a different maturity date, or offer a different rate of interest.

## Action Plan

**Step One:** Review your investment portfolio, identifying winners and losers.

**Step Two:** Sell losing investments so that you can offset capital gains. If you're convinced the stock will come back, wait at least thirty-one days and buy back some shares. Or buy a new block of shares to lock in the current low price, wait thirty-one days, and then sell the original shares.

**Step Three:** If you have bought shares in the same company or mutual fund at different times and have kept accurate records, you can identify which specific shares to sell. By selling appreciated shares purchased at the highest price, you pay less in capital-gains tax.

**Step Four:** Match short-term losses against short-term gains, long-term losses against long-term gains.

**Step Five:** Apply excess capital losses, up to $3,000 a year, against ordinary income. Additional amounts may be carried forward to future tax years.

### Buying Fund Shares

If you are considering adding to your investment portfolio before year-end, be mindful of annual capital-gains distributions from mutual funds (see Chapter 9). These distributions, generally announced in December, are taxable income even though they do not put cash in your pocket. You can keep your tax bill down by finding out the planned distribution date and making your purchase after it instead of before.

This is what can happen if you misjudge the purchase date: You buy two hundred shares of a stock fund at $60 per share on December 10. The next week, the fund declares a capital-gains distribution of $8 per share. As a result, you have an immediately taxable gain of $1,600. The $1,600 will add to your cost basis in the fund and reduce any profit when you sell—but that's small consolation because (1) you may not sell for many years, while the $1,600 is taxable now, and (2) you may not have a profit when you sell.

## Last-minute Strategies

December is your last chance to take advantage of some tax-saving maneuvers described earlier in this book. It's also a good time to give some thought to tax strategies for the year ahead.

For example: If you want to take considerably more than the required minimum distribution from an IRA—perhaps because you are buying a retirement home or planning a long-dreamed-of trip around the world—remember that distributions are taxed as ordinary income. To ease the tax bite, you may want to spread the distribution over two calendar years, taking some in December and some in January. Pay attention to your marginal tax rate and, if possible, keep withdrawals below the level that will bump you into the next tax bracket.

Here are some more things you should do in December:

- If you haven't yet done so, take advantage of newly expanded contribution limits for both traditional IRAs and Roth IRAs. For 2003 you may contribute up to $3,000 plus an additional $500 under "catch-up" provisions for taxpayers age 50 and older (see Chapter 4).

- Use up flex-plan balances (see Chapter 5) because this is a use-it-or-lose-it proposition.
- If you lost your job this year, tally up all expenses related to your search for a new job (see Chapter 5). These expenses are deductible if, when combined with other miscellaneous itemized deductions, they exceed 2 percent of your adjusted gross income.
- If you used downsizing to seize the opportunity to start your own business or become a consultant—whether or not you are still employed elsewhere—decide which retirement plan is best for your new self-employed status (see Chapter 4). If you decide on a Keogh plan, it must be opened before year-end even though you have until April 15 of the following year to make your contribution for the current tax year.
- If you reached age 70½ this year, you have until April 1 of next year to start required minimum distributions from your IRA (see Chapter 6). If you wait till then, however, you will have to take both this year's and next year's distributions in the same calendar year, paying tax—at ordinary income-tax rates—on both distributions. You may want to consult a tax adviser about whether it would be preferable to take the first distribution this year.

## Timing Is All

One of the best ways to control taxes is through timing. This means taking action before the end of the year, as discussed in the preceding section, to reap tax breaks before they expire. It also means, if possible, adjusting income and expenditures so that you can claim deductions when your tax rate is high and receive income when your tax rate is lower.

In the past, timing often revolved around the assumption that both your income and your tax rate will be lower after retirement than before. Today timing may have more to do with repeated federal tax cuts. With federal income-tax rates scheduled to decline for the next several years, pushing income into future years makes a lot of sense. Meanwhile, it's also a good idea to take as many deductions as you can while taxes are at a higher rate and the deductions are worth more.

This ties in neatly with "bunching" deductions—and December is the last opportunity for procrastinators to decide whether bunching is a workable strategy. As discussed in Chapter 1, taking as many deductions as possible in alternate years may allow you to claim more in itemized deductions in those years while taking the smaller standard deduction every other year. If you are close to the standard deduction level, now is the time to do some calculations. For example, you may be able to claim itemized deductions this year if you:

- mail your January mortgage payment in December so that the interest deduction can be taken in the current year
- prepay first-quarter real estate taxes in December
- make the last quarterly *state* (not federal) estimated tax payment for the current year, without waiting for the January due date
- have elective medical and dental work done this month instead of waiting until January, if doing so will boost medical expenses over the 7.5 percent of AGI threshold and allow you to claim a deduction

Deferring income is more difficult, although you can mail invoices late in December if you are self-employed, so that payment isn't received until the new year. Just be sure your clients are stable before you try this tactic—one corporate consultant delayed an invoice from October to December and lost out on a major fee because his client declared bankruptcy.

Most wage earners can't do much to control the timing of income, but consider the following:

1. Ask your employer to defer payment of a bonus until January, so that it will be taxed in the following year.
2. Split major IRA withdrawals in two, between December and January, if you take more than the minimum required distribution in order to make a major purchase.
3. Invest in a Treasury bill or certificate of deposit maturing in one year or less because interest is not taxable until the bill or CD matures—this is a good move to make as early as August or September, but can be made later in the year as well.

## Alternative Minimum Tax

The conventional advice to defer income and accelerate deductions fails completely if you fall into the clutches of the tax demon known as the alternative minimum tax or AMT.

The AMT was originally designed to eliminate tax loopholes for the rich but is catching more and more middle-income taxpayers in its net. The number of affected taxpayers doubled from 2000 to 2003, reaching almost 3 million households. But the damage has just begun. By 2010, the Treasury Department estimates that approximately 35 million taxpayers—one-quarter of all taxpayers and more than one-half of all those with an AGI *under* $100,000—will be paying tax at the higher AMT rate. And that could mean you.

You have to pay the AMT if it produces a higher tax bill than the regular income tax system. This can happen in several ways:

1. Tax rates and exemptions are indexed to inflation under the regular income-tax system but are not indexed for the AMT.

2. Under the AMT, you lose most of the deductions that would otherwise reduce your tax bill.

3. Scheduled rate reductions under the 2003 legislation cut regular taxes and are expected to push more taxpayers into the clutches of the AMT.

## AMT Rules

The AMT is a separate and parallel system. If there is even a possibility that you will owe the minimum tax, you must calculate your tax bill according to both regular income-tax rules and AMT rules—don't even think about the time this takes—and then pay whichever is more.

For purposes of the AMT, income is taxed at 26 percent on the first $175,000 and 28 percent thereafter. At first glance, these rates are lower than ordinary income-tax rates topping out at 35 percent, but—because there are no personal exemptions or standard deductions under the AMT—the actual tax bite is greater.

The loss of deductions is the real killer. The real estate taxes and state and local income taxes that are normally deductible are called "tax preference items" and added back into your income to calculate the AMT. It gets worse: State tax refunds are a preference item. Miscellaneous itemized deductions are ruled out. The interest on a home equity loan may not be deductible. And, in order to be deductible, medical expenses must exceed 10 percent of adjusted gross income instead of the usual 7.5 percent.

To add insult to injury, some income escapes regular income tax but is counted toward the AMT. For example, the interest on most municipal bonds is exempt from federal income tax and from state income tax for residents of the issuing state. But interest on so-called private-purpose municipal bonds is subject to the AMT. This category includes many bonds issued to finance housing, industrial development, pollution control, and airport construction.

Here's one more: Employee stock options became a nightmare for many taxpayers when the dot-com bubble burst. They are a nightmare times two for people subject to the AMT because the value of incentive stock options is income for AMT purposes—even if the stock value drops and no gain is actually realized.

Instead of personal exemptions and deductions, there is a flat exemption under the AMT. Congress has been talking for years about eliminating—or at least, drastically updating—the AMT. Instead, tax legislation in 2001 and again in 2003 increased the AMT exemption, but only temporarily. In the most recent version, the exemption is $40,250 for single taxpayers and $58,000 for married taxpayers filing jointly—but only for two years. After 2005, the pre-2001 exemption levels of $33,750 for singles and $45,000 for married couples return. In any case, exemptions begin to phase out for single taxpayers at $112,500 and at $150,000 for married taxpayers filing jointly. Exemptions disappear entirely for singles at $273,000 and for married couples at $382,000.

## Caught by the AMT

You don't have to be a millionaire to be trapped by the AMT. Far from it. More than 60 percent of the taxpayers paying the AMT for tax year 2000 reported adjusted gross income of less than $200,000. Almost half of the total reported AGI under $100,000.

One Midwestern family with taxable income of $83,000, ten children, large medical expenses—and no tax preference items—owed more than $1,000 extra in a single year because their twelve personal exemptions and deductible medical expenses were added back into their taxable income. The family took the case to court, arguing that the AMT discriminated against their religious belief that large families are a blessing. The IRS won the case.

Large families are not the only trigger for the AMT. Because state and local income tax is added back into income, residents of high-tax states such as New York and California are particularly vulnerable to the AMT. One family owed an additional $2,700 in tax because reimbursed business expenses along with state and local taxes were added back into their income for purposes of the AMT. This family also went to the tax court, and lost. As the states raise taxes to cope with budget deficits in the wake of federal tax cuts, the AMT problem will only get worse.

Investors with sizable dividend income and capital gains are also vulnerable. What counts is the amount of regular tax paid on total income. If that regular tax is reduced due to the lower rate on capital gains and dividends, you are more vulnerable to the AMT. If your income is high enough to eliminate the AMT exemption, you could wind up paying an effective 21.5 percent or 22 percent on capital gains and dividends.

## Action Plan

You can't avoid the AMT. But you can try to minimize its impact.

**Step One:** Take a second look at any investments you may have in municipal bonds and bond funds. Skip individual issues of private-purpose bonds and, if you are a mutual fund investor, read the prospectus carefully before you invest. Many municipal bond funds include taxable issues to boost the yield—but the additional tax you will owe if you are thrust into the AMT may eliminate any advantage in receiving higher interest.

**Step Two:** If you are likely to fall into the AMT trap in alternate years, bunch deductible items in the years when you can pay

## Action Plan

regular income tax. For example, you might make five payments of real estate tax in one year—the four scheduled quarterly payments plus a prepayment of the first quarter for the next year. Then pay only three installments in the year you might have to pay the AMT.

**Step Three:** If you have any hint that the AMT will affect you, meet with a tax adviser before year-end. A good tax adviser should be able to recommend steps that will minimize the impact of the AMT.

## Year-end Charitable Gifts

Many taxpayers engage in a year-end check-writing scramble in response to the deluge of charitable bids flooding December mailboxes. While it's true that these charitable donations are deductible if you itemize deductions on your federal income-tax return—and may be deductible even with the standard deduction if pending legislation sees the light of day—there are better and more tax-advantageous ways to go about supporting your favorite causes.

You may want to double up contributions in alternate years, as an example, to enable itemized deductions while making more of an impact for your favorite charity. This is a particularly wise move if you may be subject to the AMT in alternate years. In AMT years, the maximum charitable deduction is worth only 28 percent, while in non-AMT years it may be worth as much as 35 percent. That's the difference between a deduction of $280 and a deduction of $350 on a $1,000 contribution for someone in the top bracket.

You can do even better by donating appreciated assets instead of cash. If you have a gain on securities, for example, you benefit twice by donating the shares to charity: You get a current income-tax deduction for the full market value of the securities. And you bypass capital-gains tax by donating the securities themselves rather than selling them and donating the cash proceeds. If you have a loss, selling the losers and donating the proceeds to charity lets you claim both a capital loss and a charitable deduction. You can give assets outright—or you can use a vehicle such as a donor-advised fund or a charitable remainder trust, described below.

## Follow the Rules

However you choose to give, be sure to follow the very specific rules laid out by the IRS. First, contributions are deductible if they are made to a nonprofit charitable, religious, or educational organization recognized by the IRS. Contributions are *not* generally deductible when made to a political campaign, lobbying organization, fraternal group, professional or social club, civic league, homeowners association, or foreign charitable entity. If in doubt, ask the charity its status.

There are also limits on the amount of the deduction. Contributions of cash are deductible up to 50 percent of your adjusted gross income; contributions of appreciated property are deductible up to 30 percent of AGI. Give more and you may carry the excess forward to each of five succeeding tax years. Sound like a lot? You don't have to be a millionaire to find yourself in the position of giving more than half your income to charity. When a flea market shopper paid $15 for a ceramic jar, she didn't expect it to be—as it was—a fine example of eighteenth-century American folk art valued at $90,000. The jar was too valuable to sit on the coffee table, but selling it, with capital-gains tax on collectibles at 28 percent, would produce a hefty tax bill. Donating it to charity yielded a deduction for the

$90,000 value minus the $15 purchase price but—since the purchaser earned an annual income of under $70,000—the deduction definitely had to be taken over several years.

Higher-income taxpayers may be able to take more of such a mammoth deduction in a single year, but they lose out on another front because those with AGI over a certain level—starting at $139,500 for the 2003 tax year—face a phaseout on itemized deductions.

## More IRS Rules

Some charity-related items are never deductible:

1. Forget about claiming the time you put in—although you may deduct mileage and other expenses incurred in connection with volunteer activities.
2. Donations of blood are never deductible.
3. Amounts paid to purchase raffle tickets are not deductible, even if the charity would otherwise qualify for a deduction.

Contributions by check are deductible in the year you mail the check, even if it is not deposited until the following year. Contributions made by credit card are deductible in the year you make the charge. Contributions of property are deductible upon receipt; if you want to transfer securities for a deduction this year, be sure the transfer is complete before year-end.

The IRS is very particular about documentation for charitable deductions. Keep your canceled checks and receipts. And keep the written acknowledgments that charitable organizations must provide for donations of $250 or more. Charities have gotten pretty good about this. But, if you don't want to worry about collecting written substantiation, you may send smaller checks to the same charity at different times during the year. Each donation is treated as a separate item, so acknowledgment will not be required.

If you receive any benefit in exchange for your contribution, the organization must tell you how much the benefit is worth and how much of your contribution is deductible. If you pay $300 to attend a charity dinner, for example, the organization may tell you that the dinner is worth $50 and your deduction is therefore $250. But if $75 buys you a museum membership with free admission, free parking, and discounts at the gift shop, you may deduct the entire $75.

## Giving Goods

Contributions of tangible property—such as clothes to a thrift shop, books to a hospital, or a collection of baseball cards to a sports museum—fall under slightly different rules. If you donate more than $500 worth in a single year, to one or more charities, you must attach Form 8283 to Schedule A of your Form 1040. If your contribution is valued at more than $5,000—whether it is real estate, an art collection, or an automobile—you must secure an independent appraisal and attach it to your tax return. The cost of the appraisal itself is not deductible but may be claimed as a miscellaneous itemized deduction on Schedule A of your federal income-tax return to the extent—you remember the mantra—that miscellaneous deductions, as a group, exceed 2 percent of AGI.

You don't need an appraisal for publicly traded securities, because their value is readily ascertained, but you do need to have held the securities for more than twelve months in order to claim their fair market value as a deduction. Securities donated after being owned for twelve months or less are deducted at either the fair market value or cost basis, whichever is less.

There's another set of rules involving tangible assets given to charity. You may deduct the asset's fair market value—but only if the organization uses the gift in a way related to the organization's charitable purpose. If not, the deduction is limited to your cost basis, which may be lower than the fair market value. Translation: Give a painting to a museum and the current fair market value of the painting may be deducted if the museum displays the painting for at least two years. The deduction is limited to your cost basis (purchase price plus related transaction costs) if the museum sells the painting to raise money for its endowment fund.

But you're not limited to giving artwork to museums, so long as the receiving organization can use the art in some way related to its purpose. As an example, that might mean hanging paintings to cheer children in a hospital's pediatric wing.

## CARS TO CHARITY

Be doubly careful when donating a used automobile to charity. The IRS is scrutinizing such donations, looking for:
- **inflated values** assigned to junkers
- **charities selling** the vehicles instead of using them
- **middlemen collecting** cars for charities

## Gift-giving Strategies

If you have larger sums to give, consider one of the following. With each of these strategies, the charitable donation escapes estate tax at your death. Each also has its own immediate advantages.

**Donor-advised funds** pool contributions from many people and invest the money under professional management toward future charitable gifts recommended by the donors. Your contributions are immediately deductible, even if you delay making charitable gifts. Donor-advised funds are sponsored by community foundations and by investment companies such as Vanguard and Fidelity.

**Pooled-income funds** pool contributions from many donors to a charitable organization, paying annual income to the donors based on investment performance. Donors also receive an immediate deduction based upon the difference between their continuing interest in the fund and the fair market value of the donated property.

**Charitable remainder trusts** are funded with an irrevocable contribution, typically of appreciated stock that the trust sells to reinvest in income-producing securities. Because the trust sells the stock, you do not owe capital-gains tax on the transaction. You receive income from the trust during your lifetime—your choice of either a predetermined fixed amount or a percentage of the trust's value each year—with the balance going to your chosen charity at your death. You receive a current income-tax deduction based on your life expectancy and the projected gift to charity at your death.

**Charitable lead trusts** are the flip side of charitable remainder trusts. With a CLT, you transfer assets to the trust, the trust pays annual income to your designated charity for a specified period of years, and the remainder then goes to your chosen beneficiary. You might use a CLT to make a multiyear pledge to your college, for example, while leaving the balance in the trust to your children. Because the gift is deferred—your children receive the balance only when the term of the trust ends—the gift is discounted for tax purposes. As a result, more of your estate-tax exemption is preserved for other assets. Since that exemption is currently $1.5 million, and is scheduled to rise over the next several years, charitable lead trusts are for the truly wealthy who are philanthropically inclined. Jacqueline Kennedy Onassis used a charitable lead trust as part of her estate plan.

# Year-end Family Gifts

Gifts to family members generally don't do much to reduce your income tax—instead they are designed to reduce potential estate tax. One exception is contributions to the college savings plans known as 529 plans. Making such gifts before year-end can lower your *state* income tax under some circumstances. You must live in a state offering a tax break on its college savings plan. And, of course, you must live in a state with an income tax. See Chapter 8 for more detail on college savings plans.

Gifts to family members, as discussed in Chapter 6, can remove assets along with future appreciation on those assets from your taxable estate. If your estate may be large enough to be subject to federal estate tax, gifting during life is a wise move.

Many parents give their children securities, but other valuable property should be considered as well. A childless schoolteacher in New York, with an eye for art, bought inexpensive paintings from local artists over the years. Some of the paintings became more valuable as the artists became better known. When the widow had been retired for several years, she decided to minimize possible estate taxes by giving paintings to favorite nieces and nephews. Since tax-exempt gifts of up to $11,000 apiece may be made to an unlimited number of people each year, the widow was able to give half a dozen paintings to as many relatives. By making gifts during life, she got the artwork out of her taxable estate (together with the hassle of having it appraised for estate-tax purposes)—and had the joy of seeing how much the younger generation enjoyed the gifts.

## Action Plan

**Step One:** Determine if your estate may be subject to federal estate tax. In 2004 and 2005, only estates in excess of $1.5 million will face tax. In calculating the potential value of your estate, include the current fair market value of your home, life insurance, and retirement plans.

**Step Two:** If your estate may be subject to tax, think about assets you may want to give away during life. Giving appreciating assets removes both the current value and future appreciation from your potentially taxable estate.

And that's the story—or at least a synopsis of our complicated tax laws. The real message is this: You don't need to be overwhelmed by the whole tax mess. Start early, plan ahead, keep your records in order, follow the step-by-step action plans throughout *The Procrastinator's Guide*—and you can win the tax game.

## TAX TIPS FOR DECEMBER

- **December is the last chance** for procrastinators to reduce taxes for the year.
- **Sell losing investments** to offset tax on investment gains.
- **Accelerate deductions and defer income**—unless you must pay the Alternative Minimum Tax.
- **Consider charitable gifts** to produce deductions and reduce adjusted gross income.
- **Make lifetime gifts** to family to reduce your potentially taxable estate.
- **Think ahead**—and you can lower your taxes for years to come.

# APPENDIX A

## For More Information

Here are some books, IRS publications, and Web sites that can help you get organized, pay taxes, save money, and—when necessary—fight the IRS.

## Books

Apolinsky, Harold, and Stewart H. Welch III. *J. K. Lasser's New Rules of Estate and Tax Planning*. New York: John Wiley & Sons, 2002.

Berry, Richard J., Jr., Michael B. Kennedy, and Bernard S. Kent. *PricewaterhouseCoopers Guide to the New Tax Rules*. New York: John Wiley & Sons, 2003.

Bove, Alexander A., Jr. *The Complete Book of Wills, Estates & Trusts*. New York: Henry Holt and Company, 2000.

Block, Julian. *Year Round Tax Savings*. Larchmont, NY. Published annually and available from the author, 3 Washington Square, #1-G, Larchmont, NY 10538.

Carter, Gary W. *J. K. Lasser's Taxes Made Easy for Your Home-Based Business*. New York: John Wiley & Sons, 2001.

Clifford, Denis. *Estate Planning Basics*. Berkeley, CA: Nolo, 2001.

Daily, Frederick W. *Stand Up to the IRS*. Berkeley, CA: Nolo, 2001.

Daily, Frederick W. *Surviving an IRS Tax Audit*. Berkeley, CA: Nolo, 1999.

DeJong, David S., and Ann Gray Jakabcin. *J. K. Lasser's Year-Round Tax Strategies*. New York: John Wiley & Sons, 2001.

Doane, Randall C., and Rebecca G. Doane. *Death and Taxes: The Complete Guide to Family Inheritance Planning*. Athens, OH: Swallow Press/Ohio University Press, 1998.

*The Ernst & Young Tax Guide*. New York: John Wiley & Sons, annual.

Gallea, Anthony M. *The Lump Sum Advisor*. New York: New York Institute of Finance/Prentice Hall, 1999.

Hurley, Joseph F. *The Best Way to Save for College: A Complete Guide to 529 Plans*. Pittsford, NY: Savingforcollege.com, LLC, 2003.

Jacksack, Susan M. *CCH Business Owner's Toolkit Tax Guide 2003*. Riverwoods, IL: CCH Incorporated, 2003.

*J. K. Lasser's Your Income Tax*. New York: John Wiley & Sons, annual.

Lewis, Roy A., and Selena Maranjian. *The Motley Fool's Investment Tax Guide*. Alexandria, VA: The Motley Fool, 2001.

McCaffery, Edward J. *Taxing Women*. Chicago: University of Chicago Press, 1997.

Pederson, Daniel J. *Savings Bonds: When to Hold, When to Fold and Everything In-Between*. Traverse City, MI: Sage Creek Press, 1999.

Rottenberg, Dan. *The Inheritor's Handbook*. Princeton, NJ: Bloomberg Press, 1999.

Slott, Ed. *The Retirement Savings Time Bomb . . . and How to Defuse It*. New York: Viking, 2003.

Thomas, Kaye A. *Capital Gains, Minimal Taxes*. Lisle, IL: Fairmark Press, 2001.

Weinstein, Grace W. *The Complete Idiot's Guide to Tax-Free Investing*. New York: Alpha Books, 2000.

Weinstein, Grace W. *Financial Savvy for the Self-Employed*. New York: Henry Holt, 1996.

Weinstein, Grace W. *J. K. Lasser's Winning with Your 401(k)*. New York: John Wiley & Sons, 2001.

Weltman, Barbara, Esq., *J. K. Lasser's Tax Savings in Your Pocket*. New York: John Wiley & Sons, 2002.

# IRS Publications

Many of these publications may be downloaded from the IRS Web site (www.irs.gov). All may be obtained free of charge by calling the IRS toll-free (1-800-829-3676).

- Publication 1, "Your Rights as a Taxpayer"
- Publication 17, "Tax Guide for Individuals," is published for each tax year and provides basic information needed for filing that year's federal income-tax returns
- Publication 502, "Medical and Dental Expenses"
- Publication 503, "Child and Dependent Care Expenses"
- Publication 504, "Divorced or Separated Individuals"
- Publication 523, "Selling Your Home"
- Publication 529, "Miscellaneous Deductions"
- Publication 550, "Investment Income and Expenses"
- Publication 556, "Examination of Returns, Appeal Rights and Claims for Refund"
- Publication 575, "Pension and Annuity Income"
- Publication 590, "Individual Retirement Arrangements"
- Publication 929, "Tax Rules for Children and Dependents"
- Publication 950, "Introduction to Estate and Gift Taxes"
- Publication 970, "Tax Benefits for Education"

# Web Sites

- www.irs.gov is the official IRS site, offering tax forms and publications
- www.taxsites.com/state.html for information from state and local tax authorities
- www.taxweb.com has links to a range of tax resources
- www.UncleFed.com offers tax tips and audit-proofing strategies
- www.nolo.com is a site run by self-help legal publishers Nolo Press

- www.findlaw.com directs users to other legal sites on the Web
- www.finance.cch.com, from tax publishers CCH Incorporated, has informative articles and interactive calculators
- www.ici.org for information about mutual funds
- www.irahelp.com for advice on Individual Retirement Accounts
- www.bondinformer.com for information on U.S. savings bonds
- www.savingforcollege.com to compare and evaluate 529 plans

# APPENDIX B

## Tax Talk

**Above-the-line deductions.** Specific deductions subtracted from gross income in order to calculate adjusted gross income. Examples include deductible IRA contributions and alimony payments.

**Adjusted gross income (AGI).** Total income minus adjustments for above-the-line deductions. AGI determines eligibility for many tax benefits.

**Alternative minimum tax (AMT).** A parallel income tax that is calculated without some tax deductions applying under the regular income tax. Where the AMT may apply, tax must be figured both ways and the higher amount paid.

**Backup withholding.** A method used to ensure that tax is paid. If you fail to provide your taxpayer identification number (for individuals, the TIN is the Social Security number) to an institution paying interest, dividends, or other unearned income, the institution must withhold tax at the rate of 28 percent and send it directly to the federal government.

**Capital gain or loss.** The profit or loss from selling assets at more or less than the original cost basis.

**Capital-gains tax.** The tax imposed on profits from the sale of assets. The tax on capital gains is lower than the tax on ordinary income when assets have been held for more than twelve months before being sold.

**Cost basis.** The purchase price of an asset plus transaction costs (such as commissions) associated with the purchase.

**Depreciation.** A method of systematically taking deductions over time for assets—such as investment real estate or a home office—specified in tax law.

**Earned income.** Compensation—including wages, salaries, and tips—for services rendered in a trade or business.

**Estimated tax payments.** Quarterly tax payments that must be sent directly to the IRS on income where tax is not withheld.

**Fair market value.** What a willing buyer would pay to a willing seller when the transaction is voluntary.

**Generation-skipping transfer tax (GST).** A special tax on a gift or bequest that skips a generation (e.g., goes from grandparent to grandchild) and is worth more than a specified amount (the lifetime exemption in 2003 is $1.12 million).

**Gross income.** Total income from all sources, before deductions.

**Head of household.** The tax status of an unmarried individual who maintains a household for one or more dependents.

**Itemized deductions.** Specific items—including interest, charitable contributions, unreimbursed medical expenses, and taxes—that are subtracted from adjusted gross income to arrive at taxable income. Itemized deductions (when taken in place of the standard deduction) may be claimed on Schedule A of Form 1040.

**Kiddie tax.** The popular term for the tax on the investment income of children under age 14. The kiddie tax is applied at the parents' marginal tax rate on children's investment income in excess of $1,500.

**Marginal tax rate.** The tax on the top dollar of income in a graduated income-tax system.

**Qualified plan.** A retirement plan that meets federal requirements and is therefore entitled to tax benefits.

**Rollover.** A distribution from a qualified plan that retains tax benefits because it is reinvested in another qualified plan or an IRA within sixty days.

**Standard deduction.** The basic amount taxpayers can deduct without claiming itemized deductions. The amount is adjusted each year for inflation.

**Taxable income.** Gross income reduced first by deductions allowed in reaching adjusted gross income, then further reduced by personal exemptions plus either the standard deduction or itemized deductions. Taxable income is the amount used to calculate the tax you owe.

**Taxpayer identification number.** Either the Social Security number (for individuals) or a federal employer identification number (for businesses and the self-employed).

**Unearned income.** Income from any source other than compensation earned from employment; interest, dividends, and royalties are examples of unearned income.

**Wash sale.** The sale of stock at a loss when identical or nearly identical securities are purchased within thirty days before or after the sale. Capital losses generated by wash sales are not deductible.